First World War
and Army of Occupation
War Diary
France, Belgium and Germany

57 DIVISION
171 Infantry Brigade
King's (Liverpool Regiment)
2/8 Battalion
31 January 1917 - 31 January 1918

WO95/2983/7

The Naval & Military Press Ltd
www.nmarchive.com
Published in association with The National Archives

Published by

The Naval & Military Press Ltd

Unit 10 Ridgewood Industrial Park,

Uckfield, East Sussex,

TN22 5QE England

Tel: +44 (0) 1825 749494

www.naval-military-press.com

www.nmarchive.com

This diary has been reprinted in facsimile from the original. Any imperfections are inevitably reproduced and the quality may fall short of modern type and cartographic standards.

© **Crown Copyright**
Images reproduced by permission of The National Archives, London, England, 2015.

Contents

Document type	Place/Title	Date From	Date To
Heading	WO95/2983/8 57 Div 171 Infantry Bde 2/8 Bn Kings Liverpool Regt Jan 1917-Jan 1918		
Heading	57 Division 171 Bde 2/8 Bn Kings Liverpool Regt 1915 Aug-1916 Feb And 1917 Jan-1918 Jan		
War Diary	Brookwood, Surrey	31/01/1917	15/02/1917
War Diary	Boulogne	16/02/1917	16/02/1917
War Diary	Ballieul	16/02/1917	16/02/1917
War Diary	Merris	17/02/1917	17/02/1917
War Diary	Boulogne	17/02/1917	17/02/1917
War Diary	Ballieul	17/02/1917	17/02/1917
War Diary	Merris	20/02/1917	20/02/1917
War Diary	Estaires	22/02/1917	22/02/1917
War Diary	Fleurbaix	26/02/1917	26/02/1917
Miscellaneous	G.H.Q. 3rd Echelon, Base	06/04/1917	06/04/1917
War Diary	Fleurbaix	01/03/1917	10/03/1917
War Diary	Erquinham	28/03/1917	28/03/1917
War Diary	La Rolanderie	29/03/1917	29/03/1917
Miscellaneous	2/8th (Irish) Bn. K.L.R.	26/03/1917	26/03/1917
Miscellaneous	Defence Scheme-Brigade Reserve-Bois Grenier Sector	28/03/1917	28/03/1917
Miscellaneous	Defence Scheme-Brigade Reserve-Bois Grenier	29/03/1917	29/03/1917
War Diary	La Rolanderie	05/04/1917	05/04/1917
War Diary	Bois Grenier Sector	07/04/1917	12/04/1917
War Diary	Erquinghem	20/04/1917	26/04/1917
War Diary	Armentieres	30/04/1917	30/04/1917
Miscellaneous	Orders By Lieut-Colonel O.H. North, D.S.O. Commanding	05/04/1917	05/04/1917
Miscellaneous	Orders By Lieut-Colonel O.H. North, D.S.O. Commanding "H" Battalion	11/04/1917	11/04/1917
Miscellaneous	Battalion Defence Scheme		
Diagram etc	Diagram		
Miscellaneous	Operation Orders By Lieut Col O.H. North D.S.O. Comndg "H" Battalion		
War Diary	Armentieres	03/05/1917	03/05/1917
War Diary	L'Epinette	07/05/1917	11/05/1917
War Diary	Armentieres	14/05/1917	21/05/1917
War Diary	L'Epinette	22/05/1917	31/05/1917
Miscellaneous	Orders by Lieut-Colonel O.H. North, D.S.O., Cdmg. Appendix I	02/05/1917	02/05/1917
Miscellaneous	Enemy Raid-L'Epinette Sector-Night of 7.5.1917. Appendix II	07/05/1917	07/05/1917
Diagram etc	Plan Of Raid Sector V-A		
Miscellaneous	Orders-"H" Battalion, by Lieut-Colonel O.H. North, D.S.O., Commdg. Appendix III	10/05/1917	10/05/1917
Miscellaneous	Orders by Lieut-Col. O.H. North, D.S.O., Commdg. "H" Battalion. Appendix IV	14/05/1917	14/05/1917
Miscellaneous	2nd Line 8th (Irish) Bn, K.L.R.	10/04/1917	10/04/1917
Miscellaneous	Tactical Handling Of Platoons	30/04/1917	30/04/1917
Miscellaneous	Orders by Lieut-Colonel O.H. North, D.S.O., Comdg., Appendix VI	21/05/1917	21/05/1917
Miscellaneous	2nd Line 8th (Irish) Bn., K. L. R.	07/05/1917	07/05/1917

Miscellaneous	H Battalion	26/05/1917	26/05/1917
Miscellaneous	Orders by Major F.H. Bowring, Commdg. "H" Battalion. Appendix IX	28/05/1917	28/05/1917
Miscellaneous	Headquarters, 57th Division	30/06/1917	30/06/1917
War Diary	Armentieres	01/06/1917	12/06/1917
War Diary	L'Epinette	13/06/1917	15/06/1917
War Diary	Armentieres	16/06/1917	30/06/1917
Miscellaneous	Orders By Major F.H. Bowring Cmdg In The Field "H" Battalion 2nd June 1917	02/06/1917	02/06/1917
Miscellaneous	Orders By Lieut-Colonel O.H. North D.S.O. Commdg. In The Field "H" Battalion	06/06/1918	06/06/1918
Operation(al) Order(s)	Operation Order No. 1 By Lieut Col O.H. North D.S.O. Commanding "H" Battn	09/06/1917	09/06/1917
Miscellaneous	H.Q 171st Infantry Brigade		
Miscellaneous	Report On Minor Enterprise Night Of June 14/15th		
Operation(al) Order(s)	Operation Order No. 2 By Lieutenant Colonel O.H. North D.S.O. Commanding "H" Battn	13/06/1917	13/06/1917
Miscellaneous	Orders By Lieut-Colonel O.H. North D.S.O. Commdg. "H" Battalion	14/06/1917	14/06/1917
Miscellaneous	Orders By Lieut-Colonel O.H. North D.S.O. Commdg. In The Field "H" Battalion	23/06/1917	23/06/1917
Miscellaneous	Headquarters, 57th Division.	31/07/1917	31/07/1917
War Diary	L'Epinette	01/07/1917	02/07/1917
War Diary	Armentieres	05/07/1917	05/07/1917
War Diary	L'Epinette	10/07/1917	14/07/1917
War Diary	Armentieres	15/07/1917	23/07/1917
War Diary	L'Epinette	23/07/1917	31/07/1917
Miscellaneous	Appendix I. Report On Enemy Raid-L'Epinette Sector-Night of 3 June/1st July, 17	01/07/1917	01/07/1917
Operation(al) Order(s)	Relief Order No. 1	01/07/1917	01/07/1917
Operation(al) Order(s)	Relief Order No. 2	05/07/1917	05/07/1917
Operation(al) Order(s)	Relief Order No. 3	09/07/1917	09/07/1917
Operation(al) Order(s)	Relief Order No. 4	14/07/1917	14/07/1917
Operation(al) Order(s)	Relief Order No. 5	15/07/1917	15/07/1917
Operation(al) Order(s)	Relief Order No. 6	22/07/1917	22/07/1917
Miscellaneous	171st Infantry Brigade	26/07/1917	26/07/1917
Miscellaneous	O.C. "H" Battalion	26/07/1917	26/07/1917
Operation(al) Order(s)	Relief Order No. 7	26/07/1917	26/07/1917
Miscellaneous	Special Report-"H" Bn.-L'Epinette Sector 30th July 1917	30/07/1917	30/07/1917
Miscellaneous	H.Q. 171st Infantry Brigade	31/07/1917	31/07/1917
War Diary	L'Epinette	01/08/1917	01/08/1917
War Diary	Armentieres	02/08/1917	02/08/1917
War Diary	Rouge De Bout	03/08/1917	03/08/1917
War Diary	Cordonnerie	04/08/1917	08/08/1917
War Diary	Rouge De Bout	09/08/1917	16/08/1917
War Diary	Cordonnerie	17/08/1917	24/08/1917
War Diary	Rouge De Bout	25/08/1917	31/08/1917
Operation(al) Order(s)	Relief Order No. 8	01/08/1917	01/08/1917
Miscellaneous	Orders By Major F.H. Bowring Cmdg. In The field "H" Battn	02/08/1917	02/08/1917
Operation(al) Order(s)	Relief Order No. 9	03/08/1917	03/08/1917
Operation(al) Order(s)	Relief Order No. 10	07/08/1917	07/08/1917
Miscellaneous	2/8th (Irish) Bn. K.L.R Instruction No. 1	08/08/1917	08/08/1917
Operation(al) Order(s)	Relief Order No. 11	15/08/1917	15/08/1917
Operation(al) Order(s)	Relief Order No. 12		

Type	Description	From	To
Miscellaneous	Headquarters, 57th Division	30/09/1917	30/09/1917
War Diary	Rouge De Bout	01/09/1917	01/09/1917
War Diary	Cardonette	09/09/1917	15/09/1917
War Diary	Robermetz	17/09/1917	17/09/1917
War Diary	Cantrainne	19/09/1917	19/09/1917
War Diary	Fontes	20/09/1917	31/09/1917
Operation(al) Order(s)	Relief Order No. 13		
Operation(al) Order(s)	Relief Order No. 14		
Operation(al) Order(s)	Relief Order No. 15	15/09/1917	15/09/1917
Operation(al) Order(s)	Operation Order No. 16 By Lieut Col O.H. North D.S.O. Comdg in the Field "H" Battn	17/09/1917	17/09/1917
Operation(al) Order(s)	Operation Order No. 17 By Lieut Colonel O.H. North D.S.O. Commdg in The Field "H" Battalion	18/09/1917	18/09/1917
Miscellaneous	Appendix VI	01/09/1917	01/09/1917
Miscellaneous	Patrol Orders By Major F.H. Bowrini Commanding "H" Battalion	05/09/1917	05/09/1917
War Diary	Fontes	01/10/1917	18/10/1917
War Diary	Coin Perdu	19/10/1917	19/10/1917
War Diary	Proven Area	23/10/1917	23/10/1917
War Diary	Malakoff Area (Soult Camp)	25/10/1917	25/10/1917
Map	Map		
War Diary	Soult Camp	24/10/1917	24/10/1917
War Diary	Double Cott	26/10/1917	26/10/1917
War Diary	Fudan House	27/10/1917	27/10/1917
War Diary	Huddlestone Camp	28/10/1917	28/10/1917
War Diary	Masowin Camp	30/10/1917	30/10/1917
War Diary	Eagle Trench	31/10/1917	31/10/1917
War Diary	Louis Farm	01/11/1917	03/11/1917
War Diary	Soult Camp	04/11/1917	06/11/1917
War Diary	Zouafques	07/11/1917	30/11/1917
Operation(al) Order(s)	Move Order No. 21	18/10/1917	18/10/1917
Miscellaneous	Addenda To Move Order No. 21	18/10/1917	18/10/1917
Operation(al) Order(s)	Move Order No. 23	23/10/1917	23/10/1917
Operation(al) Order(s)	Move Order No. 24	25/10/1917	25/10/1917
Miscellaneous	2/8th Bn. K.L.R. Order For Move To Zouafques	05/11/1917	05/11/1917
Miscellaneous	2nd Line 8th (Irish) Bn. King's Liverpool Regiment Move-Warning Order	05/11/1917	05/11/1917
Miscellaneous	Headquarters, 57th Division	31/12/1917	31/12/1917
War Diary	Zouafques	01/12/1917	08/12/1917
War Diary	Proven	17/12/1917	17/12/1917
War Diary	Boesinghe	21/12/1917	21/12/1917
War Diary	Line	22/12/1917	25/12/1917
War Diary	Boesinghe	29/12/1917	29/12/1917
War Diary	Pompey Camp	30/12/1917	30/12/1917
War Diary	Thieushouk	31/12/1917	31/12/1917
Miscellaneous	Headquarters, 57th Division	01/02/1918	01/02/1918
War Diary	De Seule Camp	01/01/1918	01/01/1918
War Diary	Erquinghem	03/01/1918	03/01/1918
War Diary	Armentieres	07/01/1918	07/01/1918
War Diary	L'Epinette	08/01/1918	20/01/1918
War Diary	Wakelands	21/01/1918	23/01/1918
War Diary	Armentieres	24/01/1918	24/01/1918
War Diary	L' Epinette	25/01/1918	27/01/1918
War Diary	Water Camp	28/01/1918	31/01/1918
Miscellaneous	Headquarters, 57th Division	03/03/1918	03/03/1918

0095/29838

57 DIV
171 INFANTRY BDE

2/8 Bn KINGS LIVERPOOL REGT
Jan 1917 - Jan 1918

57 DIV JOV

171 BDE

2/8 BN KINGS LIVERPOOL REGT

1915 AUG — 1916 FEB
AND
1917 JAN — 1918 JAN ✓

ABSORBED BY 1/8 BN ✓

Army Form C. 2118

WAR DIARY or **INTELLIGENCE SUMMARY**

COMMANDING 2nd Line ...... Bn. THE KING'S LIVERPOOL REGT.

2/8 Liverpool Vol 1

(Erase heading not required.)

Instructions regarding War Diaries and Intelligence Summaries are contained in F. S. Regs., Part II. and the Staff Manual respectively. Title Pages will be prepared in manuscript.

Place	Date	Hour	Summary of Events and Information	Remarks and references to Appendices
BROOKWOOD, SURREY	31.1.17		Lieut. W. ROSS and one Other Rank proceeded overseas as Landing Officer.	
DO.	1.2.17		5 Officers, 10 Other Ranks proceeded overseas as Advance Party.	
DO	13.2.17		3 Officers, 83 Other Ranks proceeded overseas with Transport Personnel	
DO.	15.2.17		Battalion left BROOKWOOD, SURREY (24 Officers, 814 Other Ranks).	
BOULOGNE.	16.2.17	4.5 p.m.	Disembarked and proceeded to OSTROHOVE CAMP.	
DO.	16.2.17	10 a.m.	A and B Coys entrained.	
BAILLEUL	16.2.17	4 p.m.	DO. detrained and marched to Billets at MERRIS.	
MERRIS.	17.2.17	3 a.m.	3 Officers, 83 Other Ranks and Transport Personnel joined up with A & B Coys	
BOULOGNE.	17.2.17	10 a.m.	C & D Coys entrained.	
BAILLEUL	17.2.17	4 p.m.	DO. detrained and marched to Billets at MERRIS.	
MERRIS.	20.2.17	9 a.m.	Proceeded by march route to ESTAIRES.	
ESTAIRES.	22.2.17	"	DO FLEURBAIX as Divisional Reserve.	
FLEURBAIX	26.2.17		Transferred to Brigade Reserve remaining same billets and remained there till end of month.	

COMMANDING 2/8th (IRISH) Bn. "THE KING'S"

Confidential

No. F.B. 89
Date 2.4.17

Officer in Charge,
Territorial Infantry Northern Section,
G.H.Q., 3rd Echelon, BASE.

Herewith War Diary, A.F. C.2118, of this unit for month ending 31.3.1917.

[signature]
Lieut-Colonel,
Commanding 2/8th (Irish) Bn, Liverpool Regt.

In the Field,
2.4.1917.

O/c i/c War Diaries.
G.H.Q. 3rd Echelon.

Forwarded, please acknowledge receipt.

E.J. Worsley. Major.
6.4.17. O/c i/c T. Inf. Northern Section.

WAR DIARY or INTELLIGENCE SUMMARY

Army Form C. 2118

2nd LINE 8th IRISH BN. "THE KINGS" LIVERPOOL REGT.

Place	Date	Hour	Summary of Events and Information	Remarks and references to Appendices
Hewbrai	1/3/17	7.30 a.m.	Table over Right Sector – La Boudellerie – from 76. H.L.R. N. & B. Coys. Hazel line. Supports. 1 by ed. Hong Point. 1 Platoon. Boudellerie Post – 1 Platoon – Fray Post – 2 Platoon – Fry Farm. A Coy & Bren Carriers Subsidiary line – S.P. – Fray House. During night two casualties caused by own sniping Rifle of High Gun.	
	2/3/17		Several stick bombs thrown over. One man slightly gassed. Trenches wet in a very bad state – relief work required to put them right.	
	3/3/17		Line very quiet. Working parties repairing & building up breastworks & communication trenches, supports & front line. Two Coys continued clearing Mud in the trenches.	
	4/3/17		Our artillery became very active about 12.0 noon & did considerable damage to enemy front line. Enemy retaliated & damaged our front line. Blocked up communication trench Boudellerie Avenue. – & dug out second line.	
	5/3/17		Relief over left Batt. Front. In addition N. & B. Coys. Other Front, a two Platoons of E. Coy. held our front line. 1 Section of B Coy. & Rifle Farm, two Sections their H.Q. 1 Platoon "C" S. Hudson Bay Post – Platoon at the Front – Platoon D. Coy. Fry Farm. 1 Platoon D. Coy. Taschal, 1 Platoon D. Flew Farm. 1 Platoon in command Post, Bn. H.Q. Foray House.	
	9/3/17		Handed over the whole of the sector to the 4/5 L.N.L. & returned to billets at Hewbrai for the night of 9/10.	
Hewbrai	10/3/17	9.15	Moved off Caeck Route to billets at Evaucourt	

Army Form C. 2118

WAR DIARY
or
INTELLIGENCE SUMMARY

2nd LINE 8th IRISH BN. "THE KINGS" LIVERPOOL REGT.

(Erase heading not required.)

Instructions regarding War Diaries and Intelligence Summaries are contained in F.S. Regs., Part II. and the Staff Manual respectively. Title Pages will be prepared in manuscript.

Place	Date	Hour	Summary of Events and Information	Remarks and references to Appendices
Tynemouth	18/7	20/hr	[illegible handwritten entry referencing "A" "B" "C" & "D" Coys, Tynemouth, Riflemen etc.]	[illegible]
In Tynemouth	19/7		[illegible]	

[Signature]
LIEUT. COLONEL,
COMMANDING 2nd LINE 8th (IRISH) Bn. "THE KING'S" L'POOL REGT.

Ref. Map.   2/8th (Irish) Bn. K.L.R.   26.3.1.17.
Sheet 36 N.W.   ----------------------
1 to 1,000.
  10,000

1. In accordance with 171st Inf. Bde Order No. 5 dated
   24.3.17, the 2/8th (Irish) Bn. K.L.R. will relieve
   the 2/10th (Scottish) Bn. K.L.R. as Right Reserve
   Battn. in the BOIS-GRENIER Sector on 28.3.17.

2. Disposition of Battn. will be
A Coy. Capt.   Hutments H.18, C.2.8.
  H.C. Wright.
B Coy. Capt.   Subsidiary Line, under orders of O.C. 2/5th Bn.L.R.
  J.H. Riley.
C Coy. Capt.   LA ROLANDERIE Farm H.QQ H.11. C.6.4.
  T.L. Bailes.
D. Coy. Capt.   Hutments, H.11, C.5.4.
  A.H. Mayhew.
H.Q. Coy.   LA ROLANDERIE H.17, B.1.8.
  Lt. J. Waddington.

   3. Route from Billets.
      "A" Coy. - Rue des Acquets.
      "B", "C" and "D" Coys. - Rue du Piez.

   4. Times of Relief.
      B Coy. - Head of Coy. to be at LA ROLANDERIE H.17 B.1.8.
                                                            3.0 p.m.
      H.Q.   - do -   3.15 pm.
      A. Coy. head of Coy. to be at H.18 C.2.8, at 3.15 p.m.
      C. Coy. -   - do -   H.11 C.6.4 at 3.30 p.m.
      D. Coy. -   - do -   do.   3.45 p.m.

   5. March Formation.
      March formation as previously laid down must be
      strictly adhered to.

      Lewis Gun Limbers. - The Lewis Gun Limber of B. Coy.
      will not proceed past CANTEEN FARM.

   6. Advance Party.
      Lieut. J.H. Thornton and 1 N.C.O. per Coy. will report
      to Bn. H.Q. 8.30 p.m. 27.3.17 and proceed to H.Q.
      2/10th Bn. K.L.R., remaining with that unit overnight.

   7. Rear Party.
      Capt. J.N.L. Bryan and 1 N.C.O. per Coy. will hand
      over billets to incoming unit, obtaining certificate
      that they are in a clean condition.

   8. Transport Lines and Q.M. Dump will remain as at
      present.

                         (Sgd) J.H. Bradley Lieut. & Adjt.
                               2/8th (Irish) Bn. K.L.R.

         Copy No. 1 File.   No. 8. H.Q. Coy.
                  2. O.C.   9. T.O.
                  3. 2nd in Cd.   10. Q.M.
                  4. "A"   11. Sig. Off.
                  5. "B"   12. Lewis Gun Off.
                  6. "C"   13. O.C. Adv. Party.
                  7. "D"   14. O.C. Rear Party.

Appendix 5   COPY NO. 7

DEFENCE SCHEME - BRIGADE RESERVE - BOIS GRENIER SECTOR.

RIGHT RESERVE BATTALION.

1. The Battalion will be ready to move at one hour's notice by day and night.

2. One Company, detailed in orders daily, will be in readiness to move at once by day and night.

3. On the Alarm being given Companies will fall in on their Alarm Posts and await order to move.
A mounted Officer will be sent from Battalion Headquarters to Brigade Headquarters.
In the event of hostile shelling, Companies will be opened out.

On the word "MOVE" the Company detailed in Paragraph 2 will proceed at once and occupy the Subsidiary Line from CEMETARY Post inclusive to SHAFTESBURY Avenue inclusive, two Platoons moving by RUE DE CHARLES and two Platoons by No. 3 Emergency Route.
This Company as soon as it arrives in the Subsidiary Line comes under the orders of the Officer Commanding Sub-sector and its arrival will be reported at once to him at the "CARLTON".

Copy No. 1   O.C.
 "   " 2   Second in Command.
 "   " 3   O.C. "A" Coy.
 "   " 4   "   "C" "
 "   " 5   "   "D" "
 "   " 6   File.
 "   " 7   War Diary. (Original).
 "   " 8   "   "   (Copy).

                    (Sgd) J.H. BRADLEY,
                              Lieut. & Adjutant,
2nd Line 8th (Irish) Bn. "The King's" (Liverpool Regiment).

28th March, 1917.

Appendix II
Copy No. 2.

DEFENCE SCHEME - BRIGADE RESERVE - BOIS GRENIER.

RIGHT RESERVE BATTALION.

TRANSPORT. On the alarm being given from Battalion Headquarters by cyclist, Regimental Transport and Quartermaster's Departments will stand by ready to move.

Horses will not be hooked in.

```
Copy No. 1   File.
Copy No. 2   War Diary.
Copy No. 3   Transport Officer.
Copy No. 4   Quartermaster.
```

(Sgd) J.H.Bradley, Lieut & Adjutant,
2nd Line 8th (Irish) Bn. "The King's" (Liverpool Regiment).

29th March, 1917.

WAR DIARY or INTELLIGENCE SUMMARY

Army Form C. 2118

2/5 Liverpool M/139

(Erase heading not required.)

Instructions regarding War Diaries and Intelligence Summaries are contained in F.S. Regs., Part II. and the Staff Manual respectively. Title Pages will be prepared in manuscript.

Place	Date	Hour	Summary of Events and Information	Remarks and references to Appendices
Hd. Qrs. Laventie	5/4/17	10 p.m.	Relief of 2/5 K.L.R. commences in the Fleurbaix sector. Companies 'A' Coy on the right, 'D' Coy on the left. 'B' Coy the reserve for outlaying line of posts (in supp. 2/5 K.L.R.) with rest of 'B' Coy of K.L.R. in H.Q. area available to support the Bn. Relief completed by 10.30 a.m. 6/4/1917.	I
Fleurbaix Sector	6/4/17		Rest well & Home by the letter. 'D' to Fleurbaix	II
	7/4/17	9 p.m.	Rest well & billeted by the Fleurbaix sector. 2nd & 3rd K.L.R. moved to billets at Fleurbaix. Bombing parties & M. Gun Bullets were sent up to Sailly employed carrying to the forward positions of the R Line. Above reliefs of 10th Australian Infantry Brigade in Pioneering Order & Relief of 2/ Bn. K.L.R. to go into Regt H. Reserve. Aux. Brigade Recog. Elizabeth Lodge.	III
	8/4/17	9 p.m.	Bon Cos into billets Armentières.	Offs &
Armentières	9/4/17	2 p.m.	Extract from Div. Orders dated 24/4/1917. Relief being had been available to be considered for admission of list No. 306161, 306153 Pte J. Bannerman, 306302 Pte L. Holmes, 306303 Pte G. Hitchinson.	3F.

O.H. North.

Appendix I

Copy No. 15

S E C R E T.   O R D E R S
Map. Ref.   by Lieut-Colonel O.H. North, D.S.O.
Sheet 36. N.W. 4.   Commanding.   5. 4. 1917.
1/10,000.
----

(1) RELIEF.   The 2/8th (Irish) Bn, K.L.R., will relieve 2/5th Bn,
                    K.L.R., 5.4.1917, in the BOIS GRENIER sector.

(2) DISPOSITIONS.   Company.   Sub-Sector.   HdQrs.
                    "A"   THE RITZ.
                    Capt. H.C. Wright   Right.
                                          Left.   I.26.d.2.3.
                    "C"
                    Capt. T.L. Bailes   Centre.   TEDDY'S BURROW.
                    "D"
                    Capt. A.H. Mayhew   Subsidiary   Subsidiary
                    "B"   Line.   Line.
                    Capt. J.H. Riley   do.   do.
                    One Coy. of
                    2/5th K.L.R.   THE CARLTON.
                    H.Q. Coy.   ------
                    Major J.E. Smitham

(3) TIME OF RELIEF. At 20.15.   Head of Companies will be as below :-
                    "A"   H.30.a.9.5.
                    "D"   SHAFTESBURY HOUSE.
                    "C"   RATION FARM.
                    H.Q. Company will be at the CARLTON, at 20.45.

(4) MARCH ROUTE.   "A"   RUE DE CHARLES.
                    "D"   GRIS POT - BOIS GRENIER.
                    "C"   GRIS POT - LA VESEE.

(5) MARCH FORMATION. Platoons will keep well closed up.

(6) LEWIS GUNS.   Company Lewis Gun Sergeants and Nos. 1 & 2s (with guns)
                    will be at rendez-vous as in para. No 3 at 17.30.
                    Remainder of Company Teams to be there 20.00.

(7) DRESS.   Each N.C.O. and Man will carry his two blankets.

(8) TRANSPORT.   The Transport Officer will arrange -
                    (a) Two limbers per Company.
                    (b) Water-carts to be handed over to relieving
                        unit.
                    (c) Use of roads with Transport Officer of
                        relieving Unit.

(9) SIGNALLERS &   Officers in charge, respectively, will arrange reliefs
    SNIPERS.   with sections to be relieved.

(10) GUM BOOT STORES. O.C. "A" Company will detail 1 N.C.O. and 5 Other
                    Ranks to take over Boots at CAMBALOT DUMP and
                    SHAFTESBURY HOUSE, the party reporting at CAMBALOT
                    DUMP, 18.00.

(11) STORES.   All stores handed over, will be carefully checked
                    before being signed for.
                                          (Sgd) J.H. BRADLEY, Lt & Adjt.

Copy No 1 C.O.   Copy No 6 O.C. "C"   Copy No 12 Quartermaster
        2 2nd in Cd.   7 O.C. "D"   13 2/5th K.L.R.
        3 File.   8 Sig. Officer   14 L.G.O. do.
        4 O.C. "A"   9 L.G. Officer   15 Spare
        5 O.C. "B"   10 Snip.Officer   16 H.Q. Coy.
                             11 Trans.   "

Appendix II

SECRET.
Map Ref.-
Sheet 36.N.W.4.
1/10,000.

O R D E R S,
by Lieut-Colonel O.H. North, D.S.O.,
Commanding "H" Battalion.

Copy No. 2

11.4.1917.

(1) The 2/8th (Irish) Bn, K.L.R., will be relieved by 2/10th Bn, K.L.R., on the night of 12/13th April, and will proceed to billets at ERQUINGHEM (opposite back of Brigade H.Q., H.4.d 30 70).

(2) Relief will commence 9pm -
  "A" Coy 2/8th K.L.R. by "D" Coy 2/10th K.L.R.
  "B" "   "   "   " "A" "   "   "
  "C" "   "   "   " "B" "   "   "
  "D" "   "   "   " "C" "   "   "

(3) Guides will be furnished by Companies at 8.50pm as under -
  "A" Coy   MOAT F.Wk
  "B" "   BOIS GRENIER
  "C" "   PARK ROW (Entrance to)
  "D" "   SHAFTESBURY AV. (Entrance to).
Os.C. Coys will ensure that guides are thoroughly conversant with their destinations and routes thereto.

(4) "B" Coy, 2/5th K.L.R., will be relieved by a Company of 2/9th K.L.R., relief to commence 9pm. Os.C. respective Companies will make their own arrangements re guides.

(5) Billeting Party of 1 N.C.O and 2 men per Company under Captain H.S. Wilson will parade at "THE CARLTON" at 8am, 12th instant.

(6) i. All Trench Stores, Trench Maps, Defence Schemes, and necessary records will be handed over on relief. Receipts will be obtained in duplicate and one copy handed in to Battalion Headquarters.
    ii. All telescopes, patrol suits, Very Lights, periscopes and any other articles on charge of this Unit, will be brought out of line.

(7) Lines will be handed over in a clean and sanitary condition. A receipt to this effect will be obtained by each Company.

(8) Officers' Kits, Company Stores, etc, will be stacked under Company Guards at Ration Dumps by 6.30pm.

(9) All copies of Trench Map Sheet 36.N.W.4., scale 1/10,000, will be handed over to relieving unit.

(10) Companies when relieved, will march independently to new billets, moving out by the Communication Trenches used by incoming unit. Platoons will keep closed up, 100 yds between platoons.

(11) As soon as relief is complete, Companies and Specialists Officers will report to Battalion Headquarters by phone.

(12) Os.C. respective Specialist Sections will arrange relief with Os.C. respective Sections of relieving Unit.

(13) Each N.C.O. and Man will carry his own two blankets.
(Sgd) J.H BRADLEY, Lieut & Adjt,
"H" Battalion.

Copy No.1 C.O.   Copy No.6 O.C. "C"   Copy No.11 O.C.2/10th KLR
     2 File   7 O.C. "D"   12 Transpt Offr.
     3 2nd in Cd.   8 H.Q.Coy   13 C.R.
     4 O.C. "A"   9 "B" Coy, 2/5th   14 L.G. Offr.
     5 "   "B"   K.L.R.   15 Sig. Offr.
                                   10 O.C. 2/5th KLR.

SECRET.

BATTALION DEFENCE SCHEME.

FOR "H" BATTALION IN DIVISIONAL RESERVE IN RUE DELPIERRE AND ERQUINGHEM.

In the event of the alarm, Companies will assemble on their alarm posts and await orders.

Attached secret sketch map shows in detail the positions to be occupied by "H" Battalion in the 3rd Area Line of Trenches known as "G.H.Q. 2nd Line", H.22.a.7.3. to the River LYS BLANCHE H.16.b.5.7. where it cuts the ERQUINGHEM LYS Road at H.4.d.9.7.

The red dotted line on the attached Secret Sketch Map shows the continuous line known as "G"H"Q" 2nd Line" to be occupied by the Battalion.
The shaded squares on the red line indicate the positions of platoons and are marked "A" to "N"

Blue circular lines show the distribution of the line by companies.

Routes for Companies to take up their positions on "G.H.Q. Line" will be as follows :-
"D" Companies moves by Rue DELPIERRE.
"B" Company via Rue de Moulin.
"A" Coy and "C" Coy (less two platoons) will move via Rue de Biez.
BATTn H.Q. will remain as at present.

Appendix III

SECRET

ERQUINGHAM

To Armentieres
To Estaires

River Lares

A & C Coys
"D" Coy
"B" Coy
2 platoons "C" Coy
A & C Coys (less 2 platoons of "C" Coy)

Rue de Moulin
Rue de Bies
Farm de la Roland-erie

Rue Delpierre
"B" Coy
"D" Coy
Rue Delettré

Croix de Rome
FLEURBAIX

Scale 1/20,000

Appendix III

SECRET.   Copy No. 8

Ref. Map.   OPERATION ORDERS
1/40,000 Sheet 36   by Lieut.-Col. C.H. Worth, D.S.O. Comdg.
N.W.)   "D" Battalion.   Wednesday, 25.4.17.

(1) In accordance with 171st Inf. Bde Order No. 9 of
    21.4.17, the 2/5th (Irish) Bn. L.N.L. will move into
    billets at ARMENTIERES on 26.4.17 and become Right
    Brigade Reserve.

(2) Time of Move.- Head of each Coy. will pass BASPEAU
    CORNER at time stated below:-

        "A" Coy. Capt. H.C. Wright.   14.15
        "B" "   "   J.H. Riley.   14.30
        "C" "   "   T.C. Bailey.   14.45
        "D" "   "   A.H. Mayhew.   15.00

(3) Advance Party.
    1 N.C.O. per Coy. will report at Bn. H.Q. to Capt.
    H.T. Ellison at 9 a.m. 26.4.17.

(4) Guides.
    O.C. Advance Party will arrange for one guide per Coy.
    to be at Level Crossing B.5.B.95.81 at 13.00.

(5) March Formation.
    Platoons will move in file, 50 yds between platoons.

(6) Dress.
    Steel Helmets will be worn. Each N.C.O. and man will
    carry one blanket.

(7) Billets.
    Os. C. Coys. will render certificate before moving off
    that billets have been left in clean condition.
    The Orderly Officer will inspect all billets after
    Coys. vacate same and render report to Adjutant
    by 4.17.0 as to condition.

                            (Sgd) J.M. BRADLEY, Lieut. & Adjt.,
                                          "D" Battalion.

Copy No. 1 - O.C.
        2 - 2nd in Comd.
        3 - O.C. "A" Coy.
        4 - "   "B" "
        5 - "   "C" "
        6 - "   "D" "
        7 - File.
        8 - War Diary.

Army Form C. 2118

WAR DIARY
or
INTELLIGENCE SUMMARY
(Erase heading not required.)

2/8 Liverpool Regt

Place	Date	Hour	Summary of Events and Information	Remarks and references to Appendices
Nieuwkerk	3/5/1917		Battalion relieved 2/5. K.L. Regt. in L[t] Epinette Sector. Dispositions as per	Appendix I
L'Epinette	4/5/1917		Appendix I. Enemy raid our sector, no casualties on Appendix I. 2nd Lt. H.M. Barker O/C "D" Coy wounded & evacuated. One Lewis Gun destroyed.	Appendix II
	11/5/1917		Relieved by 2/5 - 2/6 Regt Return to billets in Nieuwkerk staff overflow "A" Coy Bart 2/6 Regt "A" Coy remain on outpost line	Appendix III
			under 2/5 Regt. O.C. 2/5 Batn.	Appendix IV
Nieuwkerk	14/5/1917		"C" Coy Fatigue L. Bailey Willows. "A" Coy in subsidiary line	
	15/5/1917		" " " " " " "	
	16/5/1917		" " " " " " "	
	17/5/1917		" " " " " " "	362
	18/5/1917		" " " " " " "	318
	19/5/1917		" " " " " " "	310
			" " " " " " "	243
	21/5/1917		A live parle cannot go effective into front line & Supports & Supports sector.	
	23/5/1917		Willoy Hedels reported to 10356/6/ Gdw. J. Emmerson	
	24/5/1917		10306531 Pte J. Talbot 10306363 L/Cpl J. Hillman by Army Commander	
			Nil.	

F.H. Barker
Major
Commanding
2nd Line 8th (IRISH) Bn. "THE KING'S LIVERPOOL REGIMENT."

WAR DIARY
or
INTELLIGENCE SUMMARY

(Erase heading not required.)

Army Form C. 2118

Place	Date	Hour	Summary of Events and Information	Remarks and references to Appendices
Havrincourt	21/5/19		Verbal instructions given by C.O. to be carried to others 2/5 K.S.R. at a moments notice. During period in the Bn. a Platoon of "B" Coy., assisted by HQ O.R.S., commanded by 2nd Lt. J. R. Peters, 2nd Lt. J. R. Smith, & supervised by these 2 Southern, carried out special training for Platoon action. The following points received special attention:—	
			I. Tactics of a Platoon in the attack — in both trench & lines of open warfare	
			II. Tactics employed in being held up by a strong point	
			III. Co-operation of weapons of fire and arms of the Infantry	
			IV. Lecture on tactical situation that may arise during an attack, & methods of dealing with same.	Appendix V
			Programme of attack attached, for Platoon Commanders & Platoons	Appendix V
		5pm	Order received from Brigade to relieve 2/5th Bn., relief to commence 9-15pm (See of leaving hereof.)	Appendix VI
Trescault	22/5/19		Message received that 2/Lt. A. E. Anderson has been awarded the Military Cross & No. 306063 Pte. J. Fletcher, & 306365 Pte. F. Rutledge have been awarded....	Appendix VI

Army Form C. 2118

WAR DIARY
or
INTELLIGENCE SUMMARY
(Erase heading not required.)

Instructions regarding War Diaries and Intelligence Summaries are contained in F. S. Regs, Part II. and the Staff Manual respectively. Title Pages will be prepared in manuscript.

Place	Date	Hour	Summary of Events and Information	Remarks and references to Appendices
L'Épinette	21/5/17	11.45 p	Pte. Nod Leith "D" Coy killed after returning from Patrol.	
	22/5/17		Enemy quiet all day.	
	23/5/17		Enemy quiet during the morning. In the afternoon two shells bursting the vicinity of the orderly room. Two came to billets. No casualties. Quiet evening and night.	
	24/5/17		Enemy quiet all day. Working & fatigue. Quiet day.	
	25/5/17		Heavy shower in our front line followed by a raid.	
	26/5/17	12.00	Quiet day. Heavy bombardment to the North.	
	27/5/17		Quiet day. Aeroplane in our sector. Hostile bombardment to the North.	
	28/5/17		Relief of two Lewis Gunners by L.G. of 7th K.L.R. completed by 6 a.m. Relief of Batt. cancelled on account of wind being favourable for a discharge of gas from our lines. At 10.35 p.m. wind was unfavourable & discharge cancelled. Details relieved by 7th K.L.R. officers & details	
	29/5/17		Rumcoy of Batt. officers 39. Other ranks 831.	

F. J. Boulton
Lt Colonel
COMMANDING 2nd LINE 5th (IRISH) BN. "THE KING'S" L'POOL REGT.

SECRET.   Appendix ". Copy No. 12.
                              ORDERS
                by Lieut-Colonel C.H.North, D.S.O., Cdng,
In the Field.   "H" Battalion.   2nd May, 1917.
━━

1. RELIEF.
    In accordance with 171st Brigade Order No. 6 dated 1.5.17
    "H" Battalion will relieve "E" Battalion in L'EPINETTE SECTOR
    on night of 3rd/4th May 1917.

2. DISTRIBUTION.
    Company.   Sub-Sector.   Localities.   Gaps.
      "A"   Right.   1 & 2.   A. & B.
    Capt.H.S.Wilson.
      "B"   Right-Centre.   3 & 4.   C. & D.
    Capt.J.H.Riley.
      "C"   Left-Centre.   5 & 6.   E. & F.
    Capt.T.L.Bailes.
      "D"   Left.   7 & 8.   G. & H.
    Captain A.H.Mayhew.

3. GUIDES.
    1 N.C.O. per Coy. will meet guides at 8-45 p.m. at ELEVEN-THIRTY
    SQUARE and conduct to respective Company Headquarters.

4. TIMES OF RELIEF.
    "A" and "C" Companies will leave billets 9 p.m.
    "B" Company will leave billets ... ...   9-30 p.m.
    "D" Company by arrangements between respective O.C. Coys. to be
    complete by 9-45 p.m.

5. ROUTE.
    "A" Coy - BRICKSTACK LANE, LOTHIAN AVENUE.
    "B" Coy -   DO.   DO., CENTRAL AVENUE.
    "C" Coy - LUNATIC LANE, QUALITY ROAD, PLANK AVENUE.

6. LEWIS GUNS.
    Lewis Guns will move into Subsidiary Line on night 2nd/3rd May,
    1917. Relief will be carried out during following day in
    small parties at a time.

7. TRANSPORT.
    The Transport Officer will arrange for necessary transport to
    be at "A" and "B" Coys' and Bn. Hdqrs. by 8 p.m.   "C" Coy.
    will use trench tramways and will have all stores, mess kit,
    &c. on trucks in RUE DE LILLE by 6 p.m. 1 N.C.O. and 6 men
    will accompany the stores of this company.

8. COMPLETION OF RELIEF.
    Relief Complete will be signalled "YELLOW".

9. BLANKETS.
    All blankets, rolled neatly in bundles of ten, will be handed
    in to Q.M. Stores at 7 p.m., receipts being obtained.

10. BILLETS.
    Billets will be left clean.
    1 N.C.O. per Coy. will be detailed to hand over to incoming
    unit and will obtain certificate that billets have been
    handed over in a clean condition.

11. RESERVE S.A.A., GRENADES, &C.
    The N.C.O. detailed to hand over billets will also hand over
    reserve S.A.A., Grenades, Lewis Gun Magazines, &c., obtaining
    receipt in duplicate, one copy to be furnished to Bn. Hdqrs.
    by 9 a.m. 4.5.1917.

                            (Sgd) J.H.BRAILEY, Lieut. & Adjt.,
                                    "H" Battalion.

             Copy No. 1   C.O.
                      2   2nd in Cd.
                      3   O.C. "A" Coy.
                      4   O.C. "B" Coy.
                      5   O.C. "C" Coy.
                      6   O.C. "D" Coy.
                      7   Transport Officer.
                      8   Quartermaster.
                      9   Signal Officer.
                     10   Lewis Gun Officer.
                     11   War Diary.
                     12   "   "
                     13   File.

Appendix II.

ENEMY RAID - L'EPINETTE SECTOR - Night of 7.5.1917.

About 7.30pm, enemy artillery opened very heavily far away on left flank; five minutes later putting barrage on extreme flank of Battalion on our left. During this barrage at about 8pm, Strombos Horns commenced to sound, continuing for fully five minutes. About this time clouds of what were at first taken for gas, could be seen rolling over sector under barrage, and respirators were put on in our sector. No gas, however, could be detected. The barrage was maintained on the left until about 8.30pm when a lull ensued to be followed a minute later by a recommencement on our (L'EPINETTE) sector and at 8.45pm a box barrage on localities I.5.1. to I.5.5., front, support and Communication Trenches, was in full swing.

By this time retaliation from our gunners had been obtained. At 9pm the S.O.S. went up from the front line. At 9.10pm two parties of the enemy got in, the third being held up by Lewis Gun fire.

The sector selected for the raid is held by three Lewis Guns. The right Lewis Gun held up the party attempting an entrance there. The centre team although consisting of one combatant only by this time, delayed the entrance of the second Bosche party, whilst the third team on the left although not successful in keeping the raiders out inflicted casualties to the number of four on this, the third raiding party.

After a stay of only some five minutes, the raiders returned, the retirement being followed at a very short interval by the arrival of a party from support line with the intention of counter-attacking.

At 9.35pm the enemy artillery commenced to slow down, ceasing five minutes later, and by 10pm all was quiet.

Enemy dead to the number of four - one officer, three other ranks - were found in our trench. Identifications show them to belong to the 1st Bn., 21st Res. Bavarian Regt. Orders for raid, maps showing sector and details of raid and barrage were found on the body of the officer.

Our casualties are:- Killed 5 Other Ranks,
                    Wounded 1 Officer, 15 Other Ranks,
                    Missing 1 Other Rank.

           (Sgd) E.J. Woodcock, 2/Lt,
                  I. O.,
                  "H" Battalion.

8.5.1917.

The following have been recommended for distinguished service in the above raid :-

        No.305804 Sgt E. Renshaw
        " 306083 Pte J. Fletcher
        " 306054 " F. Eastham
        " 306368 " F. Stanhope
        " 307581 L/C J. O'Donovan

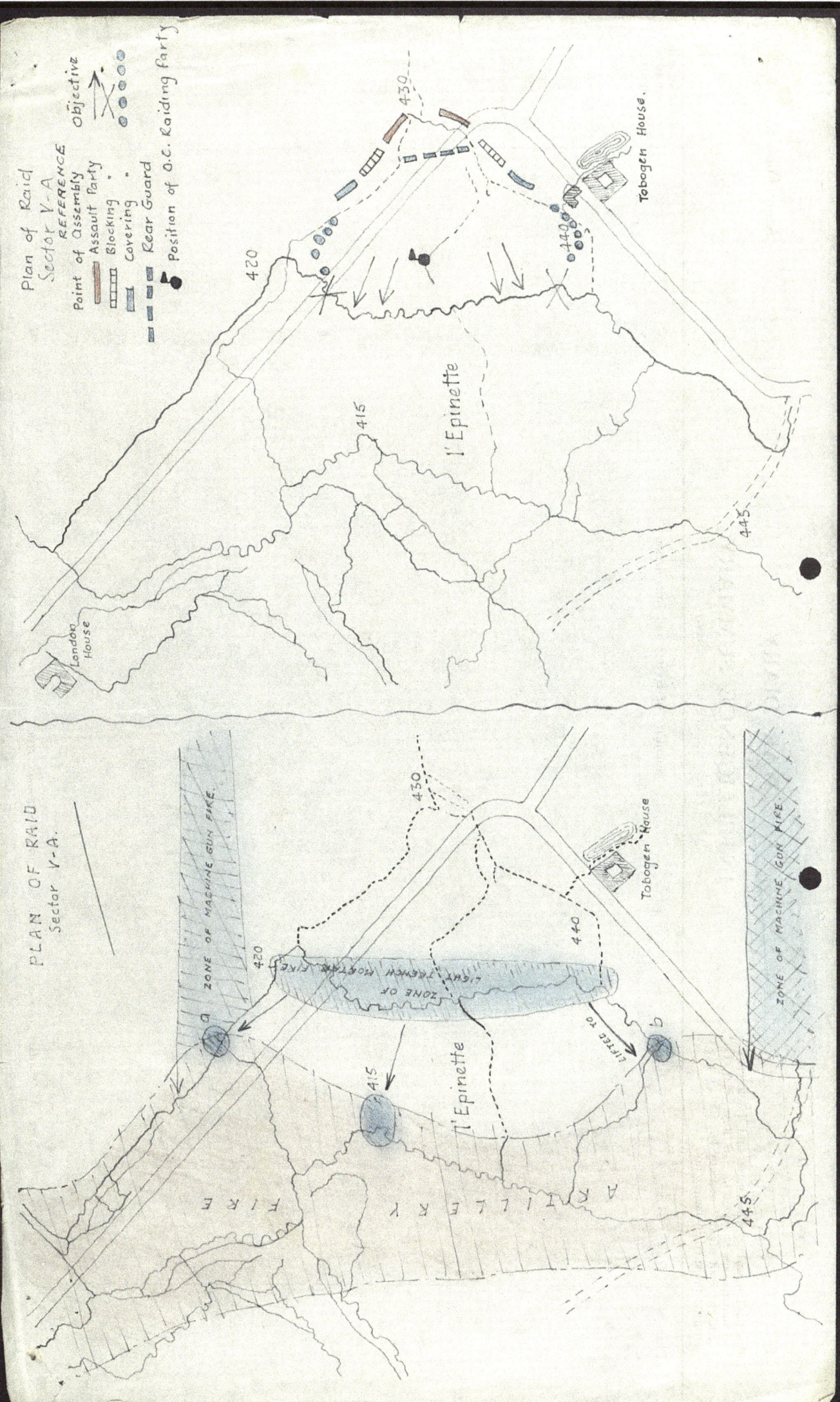

SECRET.   Appendix III   Copy No. 1.

ORDERS - "H" BATTALION,
by Lieut-Colonel O.H. North, D.S.O., Commdg.
10.5.1917.

(1) In accordance with Bde. O. No. 7 dated 9.5.17, "H" Battalion will be relieved by "E" Battalion on the night 11/12th May, 1917.

(2) Relief to commence at 9pm (i.e. time of leaving billets).

(3) Lewis Guns and Personnel of "E" Battalion will move into Subsidiary Line on night 10/11th May, 1917. Relief will be carried out at day-break on 11.5.17, in small parties at a time.

(4) "A" Company on being relieved, will go into Subsidiary Line and remain under orders of O.C. "E" Battalion.

(5) 8 Guides per Company (except "A") will parade at Battalion H.Q. at 6pm under Lieut L.H. Tilley.

(6) "B" Company will move out by BRICKSTACK LANE.
    "C"   "   "   "   " " LUNATIC LANE.
    "D"   "   "   "   " " BUTERNE AVENUE.

(7) "H" Battalion (less "A" Company) will take over billets of "E" Battalion and go in Right Reserve.

(8) All trench stores, log-books, maps, Defence Schemes and necessary records will be handed over on relief. The Sniping Officer will hand over all telescopes to incoming Unit. Patrol suits, periscopes and Very pistols on charge to this Battalion, will be handed over. Receipts in duplicate will be obtained and one copy handed in to Battalion H.Q. by 12 noon on 12.5.17.

(9) Lines will be handed over in a clean and sanitary condition. Receipt to this effect will be obtained and rendered to Bn. H.Q.

(10) When relieved, march formation will be in single file and not less than 50 yards between Sections, 100 yards between Platoons. Pace not to exceed 2 miles per hour.

(11) Officers' kits, mess equipment, etc, will be at respective dumps by 9.15pm. Medical equipment to be at SQUARE FARM DUMP by 9.30pm. Communication trenches will be clear at above times so as not to interfere with relief.

(12) When relieved Companies and Specialists will advise Battalion H.Q. by signal - "White".

(Sgd) J.H. BRADLEY, Lieut & Adjt,
"H" Battalion.

Copy No 1 O.C.   Copy No 8 O.C. "D" Coy, "E" Bn.
        2 2nd in Command.   9 War Diary.
        3 O.C. "A" Coy.   10 Lewis Gun Officer.
        4 O.C. "B" Coy.   11 Signalling Officer.
        5 O.C. "C" Coy.   12 Sniping Officer.
        6 O.C. "D" Coy.   13 Transport Officer.
        7 "E" Battalion.   14 Retained.

SECRET.　　　　　　　　O R D E R S　　　　　　　　14.5.1917.
　　　　　by Lieut-Col. O.H. North, D.S.O., Commdg.,
　　　　　　　　　　"H" Battalion.
----

(1)　　"C" Company will relieve "A" Company in Subsidiary Line,
　　　L'EPINETTE Sector, on night 15/16th May, 1917, and go under
　　　orders of O.C. "E" Battalion.

(2)　　Relief to commence at 9pm (i.e. time of leaving billets).

(3)　　Lewis Gunners will move up into Subsidiary Line on night
　　　14/15th May, relief to be carried out at daybreak, 15th May,
　　　in small parties at a time.

(4)　　Route will be :-
　　　　　2 Platoons　via　LUNATIC LANE.
　　　　　2　　"　　　"　BRICKSTACK LANE.
　　　Os.C. Coys will make their own arrangements re guides.

(5)　　Stores, Kit, Mess Equipment, etc, will be ready for removal
　　　as under :-
　　　　　"C" Company　　Coy H.Q.　　8.15pm.
　　　　　"A"　 "　　　　SQUARE FARM　9.30pm.

(6)　　The Transport Officer will make the necessary arrangements
　　　for removal.

(7)　　"A" Company will take over billets of "C" Company. Certificates
　　　will be exchanged that billets and lines have been taken over
　　　in a clean condition.

(8)　　Relief complete will be signalled "Right".

　　　　　　　　　　　　　　　(Sgd) J.H. BRADLEY, Lieut & Adjt,
　　　　　　　　　　　　　　　　　　　"H" Battalion.

　　　　　　　　Copy No. 1　Commanding Officer.
　　　　　　　　　　　　　2　O.C. "A" Coy.
　　　　　　　　　　　　　3　O.C. "C" Coy.
　　　　　　　　　　　　　4　O.C. "E" Battalion.
　　　　　　　　　　　　　5　Transport Officer.
　　　　　　　　　　　　　6　Lewis Gun Officer.
　　　　　　　　　　　　　7　File.

APPENDIX. 4A

2nd Line 8th (Irish) Bn, K. L. R.

AWARDS - OPERATIONS ON NIGHT, 10.4.1917.

MILITARY MEDALS
24.4.17.

No. 306161 L/S T. Brennand, "D" Coy.
 " 306537 Pte T. Hartnett, "D" Coy.
 " 306303 " G. Wilkinson, "D" Coy.

This N.C.O. and men rendered valuable assistance bringing in wounded from N.M.L.

Medals presented to the above by G.O.C., 2nd Army, 18th May, 1917.

APPENDIX IV.

TACTICAL HANDLING OF PLATOONS.

Four Days Course.

		Hours.
1st day -	Section Drill under Section Commander.	½
	Hand grenade throwing by Platoon.	1
	Extended order drill.	1
	Lecture showing formation of Platoon in Trench to Trench attack.	½
		3
2nd day -	Platoon Drill under Platoon Officer.	½
	Practice in Artillery Formation.	½
	Deploying from various formations, i.e. Artillery Formation, Column, etc.	½
	Formation for Trench to Trench attack.	1
	Lecture on method of dealing with hostile Machine Guns in attack.	½
		3
3rd day -	Platoon attack on trench system including demonstration of advancing under barrage.	1½
	Trench to trench attack meeting Point of Resistance, i.e. Strong Post, M.G. (hostile).	1
	Lecture on action of Platoon in open warfare on meeting Point of Resistance.	½
		3
4th day -	Attack in open warfare.	1
	Attack in open warfare meeting point of resistance showing action entailing use of Rifle grenades to give covering barrage and seizing of ground that gives tactical advantage to Machine Guns.	1½
	Action of Bombers in securing flanks and dislodging enemy in Communication Trenches.	½
		3

"H" Battalion,
30.4.1917.

APPENDIX VI

SECRET.   COPY No. 13.

                                ORDERS
                by Lieut-Colonel O.H.North, D.S.O., Cmdg.,
    In the Field.   "H" Battalion.   21st May, 1917.
----

1. Relief.
      "H" Battalion will relieve "E" Battalion in L'EPINETTE SECTOR
      on night of 21st/22nd May, 1917.

2. Distribution.
      Company.   Sub-Sector.   Localities.   Gaps.
        "A"   Right.   1 & 2.   A & B.
      Capt. H.C.Wright.
        "B"   Right-Centre.   3 & 4.   C & D.
      Capt. J.H.Riley.
        "C"   Left-Centre.   5 & 6.   E & F.
      Capt. T.L.Bailes.
        "D"   Left.   7 & 8.   G. & H.
      Capt. W.E.Jones.

3. Times of Relief.
      "A" "B" & "D" Coys. will leave billets 9-15 p.m.
      "C" Coy. will arrange relief with O.C. Coy. "E" Bn. to be
      relieved, to be complete by 10 p.m.

4. Route.
      "A" Coy - BRICKSTACK LANE, LOTHIAN AVENUE.
      "B" Coy - LUNATIC LANE, CENTRAL AVENUE.
      "D" Coy - BUTTERNE AVENUE.

5. Lewis Guns.
      Relief of Lewis Guns will be carried out at daybreak 22nd May,
      in small parties at a time.

6. Completion of Relief.
      Relief Complete, will be signalled "PINK".

7. Blankets.
      All Blankets, rolled neatly in bundles of ten, will be handed
      in to Q.M.Stores at 7 p.m., receipts being obtained.

8. Billets.
      Billets will be left clean.
      1 N.C.O. per Coy. will be detailed to hand over to incoming
      unit and will obtain certificate that billets have been
      handed over in a clean condition.

9. Reserve S.A.A., Grenades, &c.
      The N.C.O. detailed to hand over billets will also hand over
      reserve S.A.A. Grenades, Lewis Gun Magazines, &c. obtaining
      receipt in duplicate, one copy to be furnished to Bn. Hdqrs.
      by 9 a.m. 22nd May, 1917.

                              (Sgd) J.H.BRADLEY, Lieut. & Adjt.
                                      "H" Battalion.

                    COPY NO. 1   C.O.
                             2   2nd in Command.
                             3   O.C. "A" Coy.
                             4   "B"
                             5   "C"
                             6   "D"
                             7   "E" Bn.
                             8   Transport Officer.
                             9   Quartermaster.
                            10   O.C.Signals.
                            11   Lewis Gun Officer.
                            12   War Diary.
                            13   "   "
                            14   File.

APPENDIX VII

2nd Line 8th (Irish) Bn., K. L. R.

AWARDS.

BOSCHE RAID L'EPINETTE SECTOR, 7.5.1917.

MILITARY CROSS   Anderson, 2/Lt A.E.
22.5.17.   During Bosche Raid on L'EPINETTE Sector, 7.5.17, he collected all available men in support and attempted counter-attack despite barrage.

D.C.M.   No. 306063 Pte J. Fletcher, "C" Coy.
22.5.17.   Despite barrage kept up heavy fire across N.M.L., and on entrance of enemy turned gun on to 1 Officer & 2 Other Ranks, killing all these.

D.C.M.   No. 306368 Pte F. Stanhope, "C" Coy.
22.5.17.   Held up one of Raiding Parties with Lewis Gun. The Gun was hit, front part of casing flying off. Despite this Stanhope continued till gun was red hot, then going into N.M.L., found the casing, readjusted it and reopened fire.
Had 2 nights previously helped to bring in corpse killed in N.M.L.

MILITARY MEDAL   No. 306054 Pte F. Eastham, "C" Coy.
14.5.17.   In charge of a Lewis Gun team. Four of team killed at commancement of barrage, other one wounded. After assisting the latter, Eastham worked gun single handed and delayed entrance of raiders.

MILITARY MEDAL.   No. 305804 Sgt E. Renshaw, "C" Coy.
14.5.17.   Rendered unconscious at start of raid, regaining consciousness later whilst barrage was still on. Made no mention of wound but resumed command of guns of which he was in charge.

MILITARY MEDAL.   No. 307581 L/C J. O'Donovan, "C" Coy.
14.5.17.   In charge of No.10 Lewis Gun, which he kept going under heavy barrage. On Bosche entering, one came round traverse, whereupon O'Donovan tackled him, brought him down, and though wounded, held him there until another member of the team shot the raider through the head.

APPENDIX. VIII.

"H" BATTALION.

SPECIAL REPORT ON RAID - L'EPINETTE SECTOR - 26th MAY, 1917.
....

At 1-55 a.m. the enemy put a heavy barrage of Minnies, whizz-bangs and Machine Gun fire on Front and Support Line between PLANK AVENUE and JAPAN AVENUE. The enemy made for our Lewis gun in No. 5 Locality but heavy fire kept up by the number one on the gun, who reports that he saw two Germans on our wire, made them beat a hasty retreat, leaving one dead.

At 2-20 a.m. the enemy fire slackened down and by 2-35 a.m. normal conditions prevailed.

Identification was obtained from body left in our wire (photographs, letter and book) - the man belongs to the 21st BAVARIAN INFANTRY BREGIMENT 3rd BATTALION.

Photographs, letter and book forwarded.

The body is still on our wire, as it was not possible to bring it in owing to the light.

Our casualties -

                Wounded - since died   1 O.R.
                Wounded   5 O.R.

                                      2nd Lieut for
                           Major, Commanding, "H" Bn.

26th May, 1917.

Appendix. IX
14

SECRET.   O R D E R S   Copy No. 14
by Major F.H. Bowring, Commdg.
"H" Battalion.   28.5.1917.
----

1. In accordance with Bde O. No. 10 dated 27.5.17, "H" Battn. will be relieved by "E" Battn. on the night of 29/30th May 1917.

2. Relief to commence at 9.15 p.m. (i.e. time of "E" Battn. leaving billets).

xx 3. Lewis Guns and personnel of "E" Battn. will move into subsidiary line on night of 28/19th May 1917.

4. "B" Coy. on being relieved will go into subsidiary line and remain under orders of O.C. "E" Battn.

5. "A" Coy. will move out by BRICKSTACK LANE.
   "C" "   "   LUNATIC LANE.
   "D" "   "   BUTTERNE AVENUE.

6. "H" Battn. less "B" Coy. will take over billets of "E" Battn. and go into Right Reserve.

7. All trench stores, logbooks, maps, defence and retaliation schemes etc. will be handed over on relief. The Sniping Officer will hand over all telescopes to incoming unit. Patrol suits, periscopes and very pistols on charge to this Battn. will NOT be handed over.
Receipts in duplicate will be obtained and one copy handed in to Battn. H.Q. by 12 noon 30.5.17.

8. Lines will be handed over in a clean and sanitary condition.

9. When relieved, Compan-ies will move out independently, pace not to exceed two miles per hour.

10. Officers' kits, mess equipment, etc. will be at respective dumps by 9.45 p.m.
Medical equipment to be at SQUARE FARM Dump at that time.
Os. C. Coys. will each provide a loading party of 1 N.C.O. and 3 men.

11. Relief will be subject to postponement at very short notice.

12. When relieved, Coys. and Specialists will advise Bn. H.Q. by signal PURPLE.

                    (Sgd) J.H. BRADLEY Lieut. & Adjutant,
                                        "H" Battalion.

        Copy No. 1. O.C.   9. L.G.O.
                 2. 2nd in Cd.   10. Sig. Offr.
                 3. O.C. "A"   11. Snip. Offr.
                 4.   "B"   12. Q.M.
                 5.   "C"   13. T.O.
                 6.   "D"   14. War Diary.
                 7.   "E" Battn.   15. Retained.
                 8.   Coy. "E" Battn.

xx Relief (Lewis Guns) and Personnel of "E" Battn. will move will be carried out at daybreak on 29th May, in small parties at a time.

SECRET.

Headquarters,
57th Division.

....

Herewith War Diary for the month of June, 1917, with appendices thereto.

[signature] Lieut-Colonel,
Commanding, 2nd line 8th (Irish) Bn. K. L. R.

30th June, 1917.

Army Form C. 2118

WAR DIARY
or
INTELLIGENCE SUMMARY

2/8 Liverpool Regt

Vol 5

(Erase heading not required.)

Place	Date	Hour	Summary of Events and Information	Remarks and references to Appendices
Armentieres	1/9/17		Bath. Strength. Officers 36. Other Ranks 825.	
	2/9/17		Nil.	
	3/9/17		D. Coy. reliev. H.Q. form relievd "B" Coy. Coy. H.Q. Rly in	2 Appendices
	4/9/17		ammunition line.	I Ap
	5/9/17		Enemy shelling Armentieres, & in direction of Houplines.	Ap
	6/9/17		Between shelling during the day.	Ap
	7/9/17		Two new Lewis Guns. to H.Q. & to "C" Coy. of Armentieres.	Ap
			Sharp bombardment head to the north. Enemy shelling of Armentieres continued. Shelling about powerful weapon has been very severe.	Ap
	8/9/17		Relieve 7/L.S.L & R in a relief sector.	Ap I Appendix
			Shelling of back area continues.	Ap II
	9/9/17		Enemy quiet on sector.	Ap
	10/9/17		Nil.	Ap
	11/9/17		Nil.	Appendix I
	12/9/17		H.Q. & 4 Platoons. Officer 27. L.O. Epinoy. 15.OP. O.M. Nuts.	Ap II

WAR DIARY or INTELLIGENCE SUMMARY

Army Form C. 2118

Instructions regarding War Diaries and Intelligence Summaries are contained in F. S. Regs., Part II. and the Staff Manual respectively. Title Pages will be prepared in manuscript.

(Erase heading not required.)

Place	Date	Hour	Summary of Events and Information	Remarks and references to Appendices
2nd Trench	13/4/17	11½ p.m.	Lee discharged from left of our sector. Had an enemy pts north who it has found lay. Enemy shelled with rifle grds & 2" pine mortars around of midnight.	Appendix IV
	14/4/17		Lieut Entwistle 2 W. R. arrived 6 a.m. – 15 O.R.	Appendix IV
	15/4/17		Bostock shot on our ? (at 1.20 a.m. belonging to II Brenlay 19th Res. Div.) Relieved by 2/5th Batt. Reg. R.	Appendix V
	16/4/17		Nil	
Armentières	17/4/17		Nil	
	18/4/17		Nil	
	19/4/17		Nil	
	20/4/17		Nil	
	21/4/17		Capt. A. E. Heap L wounded	
	22/4/17		Nil	
	23/4/17		Relieve 2/5 W. R. O.R.	Appendix VI
	24/4/17			
	25/4/17			
	26/4/17			
	27/4/17		The ? number of observation Balloons in the vicinity has greatly increased.	
	28/4/17		? and enough pts. ? not yet invaded.	
	29/4/17		Our burial in the trenches has been fairly quiet. Enemy even ? been less of	
	30/4/17		Lillers	

O. W. Curtis

APPENDIX I   COPY NO. 8

SECRET.

ORDERS
by Major F.H. Bowring, Cmdg,
In the Field.   "H" Battalion.   2nd June, 1917.
---

(1) "D" Company will relieve "B" Company in Subsidiary Line, L'EPINETTE SECTOR, on night 3rd/4th June, 1917, and go under orders of O.C. "E" Battalion.

(2) Relief to commence at 9-30 p.m. (i.e. time of leaving billets.

(3) Route will be:-
    2 Platoons via LUNATIC LANE.
    2 Platoons via BRICKSTACK LANE.

(4) Stores, Kit, Mess Equipment, etc. will be ready for removal as under :-

    "D" Company   Coy. Hd-qrs   8-15 p.m.
    "B"   "   SQUARE FARM   9-45 p.m.

(5) The Transport Officer will make the necessary arrangements for removal.

(6) "B" Company will take over billets of "D" Company. Certificates will be exchanged that billets and lines have been taken over in a clean condition.

(7) Relief will complete will be signalled "BLUE".

        (Sgd) J.H. BRADLEY, Lieut. & Adjt.,
            "H" Battalion.

    COPY NO. 1 Commanding Officer.
         2 O.C. "B" Coy.
         3   "D" Coy.
         4 O.C. "E" Battalion.
         5 Transport Officer.
         6 Lewis Gun Officer.
         7 File.
         8 War Diary.
         9 "   "

SECRET. *war diary* APPENDIX II   COPY NO...12..

ORDERS
by Lieut-Colonel NorthO.H.North, D.S.O., Commdg.
In the Field.   "H" Battalion.   6.6.17.

1. **Relief.**
   "H" Battalion will relieve "E" Battalion in L'Epinette Sector on the night 8/9th June.1917.

2. **Distribution.**
Company	Sub-Sector	Localities	Gaps
"A" Capt. H.C.Wright	Right	1 & 2	A & B
"B" Capt. J.H.Riley	Right-Centre	3 & 4	C & D
"C" Capt. T.L.Bailes	Left-Centre	5 & 6	E & F
"D" Capt. W.E.Jones	Left	7 & 8	G & H

3. **Times of Relief.**
   "A" "B" & "C" Coys will leave billets 9-30.p.m.
   "D" Coy will arrange relief with O.C. "E" Battalion to be relieved, to be complete by 10.p.m.

4. **Route.**
   "A" Coy - BRICKSTACK LANE.
   "B" Coy.- LUNATIC LANE.
   "C" Coy - BUTERNE AVENUE.

5. **Lewis Guns.**
   Lewis Guns will move into Subsidiary Line on night of 7/8th June,1917.leaving billets at 9-30 p.m. Relief will be carried out at daybreak 8th June,1917., small parties at a time.

6. **Completion of Relief.**
   Relief complete will be signalled "THATS RIGHT".

7. **Blankets,Mens Valises,etc.**
   All blankets rolled neatly in bundles of ten, mens valises, and spare kit, will be handed to Q.M.Stores, at 7p.m. June 8th.,receipts being obtained.

8. **Billets.**
   Billets will be left clean.
   1.N.C.O. per Coy will be detailed to hand over to incoming Unit and will obtain certificate that billets have been handed over in a clean condition.

9. **Reserve S.A.A.Grenades etc.**
   The N.C.O. detailed to hand over billets, will also hand over reserve S.A.A. Grenades, Lewis Gun Magazines,etc, obtaining receipt in duplicate, one copy to be furnished to Bn H.Q. by 9 a.m. 9th June.

10. Relief will be subject to postponement at very short notice.

(Sgd)   J.H.Bradley, Lieut & Adjt.
"H" Battalion.

Copy No. 1. C.O.
2. 2nd in Command.
3. O.C. "A" Coy.
4. "   "B" Coy.
5. "   "C" Coy.
6. "   "D" Coy.
7. "E" Battn.
8. Transport Officer.
9. Quartermaster.
10. O.C.Signals.
11. Lewis Gun Officer.
12. War Diary.
13. "
14. File.

SECRET.   Appendix III
                                                                 Copy No.
                      OPERATION ORDER NO.1
                              BY
                 LIEUTENANT-COLONEL O.H.NORTH, D.S.O.
                        Commanding "H" Battn.
In the Field.   June 9th, 1917.
━━

1. INTENTION.   On Z day at Zero Hour a party of "H" Battn. will
                     raid enemy front line trench between I 11 a 35 25
                     and I 11 c 85 95.98

2. OBJECT.   1. Capture or destroy enemy.
                     2. Obtain identifications.
                     3. Destroy machine guns, technical weapons or
                        dug outs.

3. INFORMATION.   At point I 11 a 40 10 enemy front line is cut by
                        wire going from front of trench to support
                        line. M.G. said to be at point I.11 a 35 17.
                     Borrow ditch in front of enemy parapet, 3ft.6in.deep
                        10 ft. wide. Almost dry.
                     Wire of enemy in good condition from point I 11 a
                        40 10 to 15 yards to right. At the latter
                        point, there are broken knife rests, where
                        going is good.
                     Going across N.M.L. good.

4. STRENGTH OF   1 Officer, 15 Other Ranks.
   PARTY.

5. COMPOSITION   a. Right blocking party. 1 N.C.O., 3 bombers.
      OF   b. Left blocking party. 1 N.C.O., 1 bayonet man,
    PARTY.   2 bombers, 1 rifle grenadier (with fixed
                          bayonet)
                     c. Demolition Party. 1 Officer, 1 N.C.O., 2
                          bayonet men, 3 men with revolvers, knob-
                          kerries and bombs.
                     One man in each party will be told off to obtain
                     identification.

6. DRESS.   Service Dress tunic, puttees, box respirators,
                        white armlet bands, steel helmet (WITH COVER),
                        label with rank, number, name and religion.
                     Faces and hands will be blackened.
                     All possible identifications will be left with officer
                     to be detailed by "B" Company. This Officer will
                     see each member of the party individually at Zero
                     minus one hour and receive discs, letters, papers etc.
                     All ranks will wear a khaki handkerchief over the
                     white band until entering enemy trench, when the
                     khaki handkerchief will be ripped off.

7. EQUIPMENT.   Officer and N.C.O's.   Revolver, watch, torch, whistle.
                                            In addition, the officer will
                                            take Very Pistol, two green and
                                            two Red lights.
                     Bombers.   Waistcoat. 20 Mills' bombs, knob-
                                            kerry.
                     Bayonet men.   Rifle, bayonet, torch, 80
                                            rounds, S.A.A.
                     Rifle Grenadiers.   12 Mills', 25 rounds .303 special
                                            blank, fixed bayonet.
                     Each N.C.O. and man will in addition take with
                     him one packet of chocolate.

8. ACTION.   At Zero minus 20 the three parties will leave sally
                     port I 11 c 85 95, bear off to left to end of ditch,
                     then continue along old farm road.

- 2 -

8. Action.
(Continued).
   a Party bear off to right at end of ditch to knife rests.
   b Party continue to railway embankment.
   c Party to enemy trench I 11 a 30 80.

At Zero right blocking Party will take up position on enemy parapet, demolition and left blocking parties entering trench.

At Zero plus 5 all parties will leave enemy trench and make their way back to our lines.

In the event of enemy putting on a barrage too heavy to go through, parties will take cover in shell holes until the barrage lifts.

9. ARTILLERY.
If necessary, 18 pounders will put a barrage on junction of front line I 11 a 8 9 40, along C.T. to I 11 a 80 35, from this point along support trench to I 11 c 60 98, and at point ~~along support trench~~ I.11.c.60.72.
4.5" Hows. on known points of retaliation.

Artillery signal will be Green Very Light followed by Red in quick succession.

On seeing ~~the~~ THESE Lights all parties will retire from enemy line whether observed before or after zero plus five.

10. CHECKING.
O.C. "B" Company will detail one officer to check parties out on leaving sally port, and also on their return. N.C.O's in charge of parties will report to this officer immediately they return, and to whom they will report any casualties.

11. MEDICAL ARRANGEMENTS.
The Medical Officer will arrange to be in attendance at sally port at zero hour.
O.C. A, C and D Coys. will place 4 stretcher bearers and 1 stretcher each at disposal of Medical Officer.
O.C. Coy. "E" Battalion will place 8 stretcher bearers and 2 stretchers at disposal of Medical Officer.
Stretcher Bearers will report at sally port at zero hour.

12. COMMUNICATION.
Signalling Officer will arrange for two runners to report to O.C. checking in at sally port at zero minus five.
O.C. Coys. will give instructions that Bn.H.Q. are not called up on 'phone unless of necessity) from zero to zero plus 45.

13. ACKNOWLEDGE.

Sent out at   p.m.
                                               Lieut. and Adj't.,
                                               "E" Battalion.

COPY NO.	
1	Bde.
2	"
3	C.O.
4	O.C. Party.
5	Retained.
6	O.C. "A" Coy.
7	O.C. "B" "
8	O.C. "C" "
9	O.C. "D" "
10	O.C. Coy. "E" Bn.
11	Medical Officer.
12	Signal Officer.
13	War Diary.
14	" "

APPENDIX III.

H.Q. 171st Infantry Brigade.

MINOR ENTERPRISE NIGHT OF 12/13th. JUNE.1917.

A party of one Officer and fifteen other ranks left our lines at point I.11.c.05.95. at 10.40.p.m. and entered salient in enemen enemies lines between points I.11.a.35.25. and I.11.c.55.98. The enemy line being entered at 11.p.m. The trench was found unoccupied and in a very bad condition, as the result of heavy shelling. Movent was heard in travel trench some 50yds in rear. An effort was made to reach this line but it did not succedd in consequence of front being heavily wired. The party withdrew after being in the enemy line twenty-five minutes without encountering the enemy. The enemy wire at the apex of the salient consists of knife rests numbering three in depth. On right flank two or three strands of wire had to be cut, on the left flank there was no wire to cause inconvenience; but there was a burrow ditch full of water. One German stick grenade was found in the trendn.

[signature]

2nd Lieut. for
Lieut-Colonel.
Commdg. "H" Battn.

APPENDIX. IV

REPORT ON MINOR ENTERPRISE NIGHT OF JUNE 14/15th.

A party of one officer and sixteen other ranks left our lines from point I5.c.50.58. at 11-5.p.m. and entered the enemy trench between points I5.c.92.26. and I5.c.98.40. with the object of obtaining identification and encountering enemy.
The trench on entrance was found to be in a bad state of repair and unoccupied.
The party proceeded to examine trench when gongs, bells, and rattles, presumably a gas alarm, were heard. On these sounding four enemy were observed to come in from N.M.L. some 50yds. to left of party and continue up trench away from party. The latter dashed off to encounter them but their progress was impeded in consequence of the bad state of the trench, and on their reaching the point where they appeared to have come in no sign of the enemy could be seen. The party continued along the trench to I5. d. 02. 48. without any sign of enemy. The party then, about 12-10.a.m. withdrew from enemy trench and took up position on enemy parapet to await the appearance of a Trench Patrol, Still no sign of the enemy however, and the party returned to our lines at 12-45.a.m.
Large working parties were heard about X 70yds. in rear of front line, hammering and shouting.

O.M. Notts   2.Lt.

for Lt. Col. Comdg. =H= Battn.

SECRET. APPENDIX IV Copy No.........

OPERATION ORDER NO. 2
BY
LIEUTENANT-COLONEL O.H.NORTH, D.S.O.,
Commanding "H" Battn.

In the Field.   June 13th, 1917.
----

1. **INTENTION.**   On Z day at Zero Hour a party of "H" Battalion will raid enemy front line trench between I 5 c 92 26 and I 5 c 98 40.

2. **OBJECT.**
   1. Capture or destroy enemy.
   2. Obtain identifications.

3. **STRENGTH OF PARTY.**   1 Officer, 15 Other Ranks.

4. **COMPOSITION OF PARTY.**
   a. Right blocking party.
      1 N.C.O., 1 Bayonet man, 2 Bombers, 1 rifle grenadier with fixed bayonet.
   b. Left blocking party.
      1 N.C.O., 1 Bayonet man, 2 bombers, 1 rifle grenadier with fixed bayonet.
   c. Assaulting party.
      1 Officer, 1 N.C.O., 2 bayonet men, 2 men with revolvers, knob kerries, and bombs; 1 telephonist.
   One man in each party will be told off to obtain identifications.

5. **DRESS.**   Service dress tunic, puttees, box respirators, white armlet bands, steel helmet (with cover) label with rank, No., name and religion. Faces and hands will be blackened.
   All ranks will wear a khaki handkerchief over the white band until entering enemy trench, when the khaki handkerchief will be ripped off.

6. **EQUIPMENT.**

Officer & N.C.Os.	Revolver, watch, torch, whistle.
Bombers.	2 waistcoats, 16 Mills' Bombs, knob kerries, wire cutters.
Bayonet Men.	Rifle, bayonet, torch, 50 rounds S.A.A.
Rifle Grenadiers.	12 Mills', 25 rounds .303 blank, fixed bayonet.
Telephonist.	Revolver, wire, O. Mk III 'phone.

   Each N.C.O. and man will in addition take with him one packet of chocolate.

7. **ACTION.**   At zero minus 20 the three parties will leave our trench at Point I 5 c 50 58 and make their way across to enemy trench. They will take cover our side of enemy wire and enter enemy trench at zero at the following points.

   a. Right Blocking Party.   I 5 c 92 26.
   b. Left Blocking Party.   I 5 c 98 42.
   c. Assaulting Party.   I 5 c 95 32.

   In the event of trench being unoccupied, Left Blocking party and Assaulting party will proceed together along enemy trench to C.T. I 5 d 12 50 and cut off Listening Post at I 5 d 02 48, Right Blocking Party remaining at I 5 c 92 26.

-2-

Should no sign of enemy still have been seen on reaching this, the three parties will assemble at I 5 c 92 26 and wait the approach of enemy patrols.
Order to withdraw will be given by O.C. Raid, i.e. one blast of whistle, or in event of enemy barrage being put on enemy front line, one green very light.

8. ARTILLERY. If required on reaching first objective, 18 pounders will barrage C.Ts. I 5 c 75 18 and I 5 d 12 50, Support Line I 11 b 01 95 to I 5 d 10 80; 4.5's on C.T. I 5 d 12 68.06
If required afterwards, 18 pounders on C.Ts. I 5 c 75 18 I 5 d 12 50; 4.5's on C.T. I 5 d 12 68.06

9. T.M.B's. On Artillery barrage being brought down, Medium T.M.B'y will open on Support Line I 11 b 01 95.
Light T.M.B'y on C.T. I 5 d 12 68.06.

10. COMMUNICATION. Signalling Officer will arrange for telephone station at point of exit.
One telephonist will accompany O.C. Raid and will report progress to our front line by code.
Signalling Officer will arrange for two runners to O.C.
Checking In at zero minus five.
O.C. Coys. will give instructions that Bn. H.Q. are not called up on the 'phone (unless of necessity) from Zero to Zero plus 45.

11. CHECKING. O.C. "C" Coy. will detail one Officer to check parties out on leaving and also on their return.
N.C.Os. in charge of parties will report to this officer immediately they return, and to whom they will report any casualties.

12. MEDICAL ARRANGEMENTS. The Medical Officer will arrange to be in attendance at point of exit at zero hour.
O.C. "A" "B" and "D" Coys. will place 4 stretcher bearers and 1 stretcher each at disposal of Medical Officer.
O.C. Coy. "E" Battn. will place 8 stretcher bearers and 2 stretchers at disposal of Medical Officer.
Stretcher Bearers will report at Point of Exit at Zero Hour

13. ACKNOWLEDGE.

Sent out p.m.
Lieut. & Adjt.,
"H" Battalion.

Copies No. 1 Brigade.
2 "
3 C.O.
4 O.C. Party.
5 Retained.
6 O.C. "A" Coy.
7 "B"
8 "C"
9 "D"
10 O.C. Coy. "E" Bn.
11 O.C. Trench Mortar Battery.
12 Medical Officer.
13 Signalling Officer.
14 War Diary.
15 " "

SECRET.　　　　　　　　O R D E R S　　APPENDIX V　Copy No. 15.
　　　　　　　by Lieut-Colonel O.H.North, D.S.O., Commdg.
　　　　　　　　　　"H" Battalion.　　　　　　　　14.6.17.
----

1. In accordance with Bde O. No.13. dated 14.6.17. "H" Battn will be ~~rel~~ relieved by "E" Battn. on the night of 15/16th June.1917.

2. Relief to commence at 9.30 p.m. (i.e. time of leaving billets).

3. Lewis Guns and personnel of "E" Battn. will move into Subsidiary Line on night of 15/16th June.1917.
   Relief will be carried out at daybreak on 16th June, in small parties at a time.

4. "A" Coy on being relieved will go into Subsidiary Line and remain under orders of O.C. "E" Battn.

5. "B" Coy will move out by BRICKSTACK LANE.
   "C"　 "　 "　 "　　　 " LUNATIC LANE.
   "D"　 "　 "　 "　　　 " BUTTERNE AVENUE.

   "B" Coy will not commence to use BRICKSTACK LANE until rear of "A" Coy. "E" Battn. is clear.

6. "H" Battn. less "A" Coy will take over billets of "E" Battn. and go in Right Reserve.

7. All trench stores, logbooks, maps, defence and retaliation schemes etc. ~~etc~~ will be handed over on relief. The Sniping Officer will hand over all telescopes to incoming Unit. Patrol suits, periscopes and very pistols on charge to this Battalion will NOT be handed over.
   Receipts in duplicate will be obtained and one copy handed to Battn. H.Q. by 12 noon 17.6.17.

8. Lines will be handed over in a clean and sanitary condition.

9. When relieved Companies will move out independently, pace not to exceed two miles per hour.

10. Officers' kits, mess equipment etc will be at respective dumps by 10 p.m.
    Medical equipment to be at SQUARE FARM at that time.
    Os. C. Coys. will each provide a loading party of 1 N.C.O. and 3 men.

11. Relief will be subject to postponement at very short notice.

12. When relieved, Coys and Specialists will advise Bn. H.Q. by signal BLACK

　　　　　　　　　　　　　　　(Sgd) J.H. BRADLEY Lieut. & Adjt.,
　　　　　　　　　　　　　　　　　　　"H" Battalion.

　　　Copy No. 1. CO.
　　　　　　　　2 2nd in Cd.　　　　10 Sigs. Offr.
　　　　　　　　3 O.C. "A" Coy.　　 11 Sniping "
　　　　　　　　4　　　"B"　　　　　12 Q.M.
　　　　　　　　5　　　"C"　　　　　13 T.O.
　　　　　　　　6　　　"D"　　　　　14 War Diary.
　　　　　　　　7 "E" Battn.　　　　15　 "
　　　　　　　　8 O.C. Coy."E" Bn. 16 File.
　　　　　　　　9 L.G. Offr.

SECRET.

SECRET.   APPENDIX V   Copy No. 12.
                         ORDERS
                  by Lieut-Colonel O.H.North, D.S.O., Cmdg,
   In the Field.   "H" Battalion.   23rd June, 1917.
   ----

1. **RELIEF.**
   "H" Battalion will relieve "E" Battalion in L'EPINETTE SECTOR on the night of 24th/25th June, 1917.

2. **DISTRIBUTION.**

Company.	Sub-Sector.	Localities.	Gaps.
"A" Capt. H.C.Wright.	Right.	1 & 2.	A & B.
"B" Capt. J.H.Riley.	Right-Centre.	3 & 4.	C & D.
"C" Major T.L.Bailes.	Left-Centre.	5 & 6.	E & F.
"D" Capt. J.E.Smitham.	Left.	7 & 8.	G & H.

3. **TIMES OF RELIEF.**
   "A" "B" and "D" Companys will leave billets 9-45 p.m. "C" Company will arrange relief with O.C. Coy. "E" Bn. to be relieved, relief to be complete by 10 p.m.

4. **ROUTE.**   "A" Company - BRICKSTACK LANE.
                "B"   "   - LUNATIC LANE.
                "D"   "   - BUTHERNE AVENUE.

5. **LEWIS GUNS.**
   Lewis Guns will move into Subsidiary Line on night of 23rd/24th June, 1917, leaving billets at 9-45 p.m. Relief will be carried out at daybreak 24th June, 1917 - small parties at a time.

6. **COMPLETION OF RELIEF.**
   Relief complete will be signalled "DORKING".

7. **BLANKETS, MENS' VALISES, ETC.**
   All blankets, rolled neatly in bundles of ten, mens' valises and spare kit, will be handed in to Q.M. Stores, at 7 p.m. June 24th, receipts being obtained.

8. **BILLETS.** Billets will be left clean. One N.C.O. per Coy. will be detailed to hand over to incoming Unit and will obtain certificate that billets have been handed over in a clean condition.

9. **RESERVE S.A.A., GRENADES, ETC.**
   The N.C.O. detailed to hand over billets, will also hand over reserve S.A.A., Grenades, Lewis Gun Magazines, etc. obtaining receipt in duplicate, one copy to be furnished to Bn. Headquarters by 9 a.m. 25th June.

10. **RELIEF WILL BE SUBJECT TO POSTPONEMENT AT VERY SHORT NOTICE.**

                                (Sgd) J.H.BRADLEY, Lieut. & Adjt.,
        Issued at   p.m.   "H" Battalion.

        Copy No. 1.   C.O.   Copy No. 8   Transport Officer
              2.   2nd in Cd.   9.   Quartermaster.
              3.   O.C. "A" Coy.   10.   O.C. Signals.
              4.   O.C. "B" "   11.   Lewis Gun Officer.
              5.   O.C. "C" "   12.   War Diary.
              6.   O.C. "D" "   13.   "   "
              7.   "E" Battalion.   14.   File.

Headquarters,
    57th Division.

....

Herewith War Diary for the month of July, with Appendices thereto.

F. H. Bowring
                Major,
Commanding, 2nd Line 8th (Irish) Bn. K. L. R.

31st July, 1917.

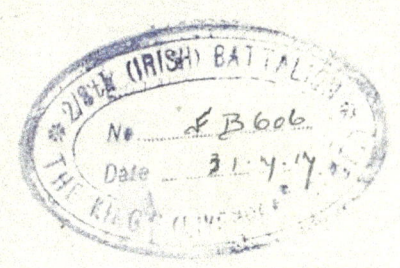

WAR DIARY
or
INTELLIGENCE SUMMARY.
(Erase heading not required.)

Army Form C. 2118.

2/8 King's (Liverpool Regt.) July 1917

Place	Date	Hour	Summary of Events and Information	Remarks and references to Appendices
L'EPINETTE	1.7.17		"B" Coy sector raided	Appendix I/VII
D°	–		Strength - Officers 29; Other Ranks 640	Appendix II
D°	2.7.17		Relieved by 2/5th Bn K.L.R.	
ARMENTIERES	5.7.17		As platoons are so small arrangements have been made to make each Coy into three platoons instead of four, there retaining the Platoon as a fighting unit &	Appendix III
			strengthening them. Where the Coys	
			"C" Coy - Captain Smithson - relieves B Coy - Captain Riley in subsidiary line	
L'EPINETTE	10.7.17		Relieved 2/5th K.L.R. in L'EPINETTE SECTOR	Appendix IV/VII
D°	12.7.17		Very Quiet period - 2/4 Bn (242 2/2 L R) heavily shelled	Appendix V
D°	14.7.17		Relieved by 2/5th K.L.R. after only four days in line.	
ARMENTIERES	15.7.17		"D" Coy - Capt. E. Smithson - go to BAC-ST MAUR for special training	Appendix VI
D°	18.7.17		"B" Coy - Capt. J. A. Riley - relieved A Coy in Subsidiary Line	
D°	20.7.17		Town heavily shelled. Considerable damage being done to billets	
D°	21.7.17		Heavy shelling continues. Gas shells mixed with HE were used in considerable quantities	
D°	22.7.17		A Coy billet being unhealthy fresh billets were obtained in the rear of the town	
D°	23.7.17	(no entry)		

Lt. Col. H. Eshing Trafford
Commanding 2nd Line 8th (Irish) Bn. "The King's" L'pool Regt.

WAR DIARY
or
INTELLIGENCE SUMMARY

Army Form C. 2118.

Sheet II.

Place	Date	Hour	Summary of Events and Information	Remarks and references to Appendices
L'EPINETTE	23/7/17		Two Coys relieved two Coys of 2/5 K.L.R. in M Line. Road to Communication Trench heavily shelled with shrapnel and gas shells causing 25 casualties in "A" Coy. – 2nd Lt Milne	APPENDIX VII
Do	24/7/17		Enemy artillery fairly active on the line	
Do	25/7/17		Enemy artillery quieter	
Do	26/7/17		Minor Enterprise by "B" Coy. Captain Smithson	APPENDIX VIII
Do	27/7/17		Enemy fairly quiet our Sector. "C" & "D" Coys relieved two coys of 2/6 K.L.R.	APPENDIX IX
Do	28/7/17	12mid to 3:30am	Heavy bombardment of ARMENTIERES with gas shells lasting 2.30am – 2/5 K.L.R. suffered heavy casualties	
Do	29/7/17		Shelling of Armentieres continued. Enemy fly on aerodromes & M.G. fire.	
Do	30/7/17		enemy drive to be aware to Lieuftrns since 12/11/17 All O.M.S. Stampfer pipes 5th Bn on the M.M. Willing L. Lancashire Contumual 2nd Bn East on the road	APPENDIX X
		9.15 am	Line set 9.45 am.	
Do	31/7/17		Owing to heavy casualties in the Bn it is to be relieved by the "D" Loos 1st Bn Dec and a gd part of the day at Ployers moving might from Sheet two they away on Sept line.	APPENDIX XI

J H Bowling Major
COMMANDING 2nd LINE 8th (IRISH) BN. "THE KING'S" L'POOL REGT.

APPENDIX I.

REPORT ON ENEMY RAID - L'EPINETTE SECTOR - Night of 30 June/1st July, 17.
....

2-10 a.m. Enemy placed a box barrage, composed of Trench Mortars, Artillery and Machine Guns on Front Line G.Gap No. 7 Locality (I.5.a.) along AUSTRALIA AVENUE, WILLOW WALK, QUAKITY STREET, PLANK AVENUE, and JAPAN AVENUE, at the same time placing a lighter barrage on No. 6 & No. 4 Locality.
At 2-15 a.m. an Enemy Raiding Party about forty strong, entered No. 7 Locality, the party being divided into three squads. The parties on entrance came into contact with two bombing posts, who, on being told to surrender, replied vigourously with bombs, whereupon the enemy withdrew, leaving one wounded on our parapet.
Enemy barrage ceased 2-35 a.m. Patrols immediately went out and searched N.M.L. but no further sign of the enemy was seen, The route taken by the enemy was easily discernable through the long grass and this was followed half-way across N.M.L. to a ditch crossed by a bridge which had been removed. Pools of blood were visible all along the track and in our trench.
Between 60 and 70 Stick Bombs were found in our trenches and in N.M.L. 3 rifles, one of which was blown to pieces and covered with blood, were found in our trench. Also 2 caps with the PRUSSIAN Rosettes on them.
The wounded prisoner who was wearing a riband of the Iron Cross and had 6 on his shoulder strap was wearing and Identity Disc with "GUSTAV KLAUKE. POLSBURG. K.r. SPREMBERG. 1ERS. BTL. GREN. R.7." on the front of it and on the back "1.K.R.1.R.6 Nr. 300."
Our Casualties were - 5 O.R. killed - 7 O.R. wounded.
Our S.O.S. barrage was in full swing in four minutes and was most effective.
A wiring Party of the 2/5th K.L.R. who had furnished work and were proceeding down the Communication Trench on hearing the enemy barrage at once returned to the front line and reported to the Trench Officer.
A large nmber of friction igniters were found in our trenches where the Germans had been throwing bombs.
Much damage was done to our front line and Communication Trenches.

F. A. Bowring Major
fr.
Lieut-Colonel,
Commanding, "H" Battalion.

1st July, 1917.

APPENDIX II
Copy No. 14A

RELIEF ORDER NO. 1
by Lieut-Colonel O.H.North, D.S.O.,
Commanding "H" Battn.   1st July, 1917.

----

1. In accordance with Brigade Orders dated 1..7.17, "H" Battalion will be relieved by "E" Battalion on the night of 2nd 3rd July, 1917.

2. Relief to commence at 9-30 p.m. (i.e. time of leaving billets.).

3. Lewis Guns and personnel of "E" Battalion will move into Subsidiary Line on night of 1st/2nd July, 1917.
Relief will be carried out at daybreak on 2nd July, in small parties at a time.

4. "B" Company on being relieved will go into Subsidiary Line and remain under orders of O.C. "E" Battalion.

5. "A" Company will move out by BRICKSTACK LANE.
   "C"   "   "   "   " " LUNATIC LANE.
   "D"   "   "   "   " " BUTTERNE AVENUE.

   "D" Company will not commence to use BUTTERNE AVENUE until rear of "C" Company, "E" Battalion is clear.

6. "H" Battalion, less "B" Company will take over billets of "E" Battalion and go in Right Reserve.

7. All trench stores, logbooks, maps, defence and retaliation schemes etc. will be handed over on relief.
Receipts in duplicate will be obtained and one copy handed in to Battalion Orderly Room by 12 noon 3rd. July.

8. Lines will be handed over in a clean and sanitary condition.

9. When relieved, companies will move out independently, pace not to exceed two miles per hour.

10. Officers' kits, mess equipment, etc., will be at respective dumps by 10 p.m.
Medical Equipment to be at SQUARE FARM at that time.
Os.C.Coys. will each provide a loading party of 1 N.C.O. and 3 men.

11. When relieved, Companies and Specialists will advise Bn. H.Q. by signal "FARNHAM".

(Sgd) J.H.BRADLEY, Lt. & Adjt.,
"H" Battalion.

Copy No.		Copy No.	
1.	C.O.	9.	L.G.Officer.
2.	2nd in Cd.	10.	O.C. Signals.
3.	O.C. "A" Coy.	11.	M.O.
4.	"B"	12.	Q.M.
5.	"C"	13.	T.O.
6.	"D"	14.	War Diary.
7.	"E" Bn.	15.	" "
8.	O.C. Coy. "E" Bn.	16.	File.

SECRET.   APPENDIX III   Copy No. 9

RELIEF ORDER NO. 2
by Lieut-Col. O.H.North, DSO., Commanding,
In the Field.   "H" Battalion.   6th July, 1917.

(1)   "D" Company will relieve "B" Company in Subsidiary Line,
        L'EPINETTE SECTOR, on night 6th/7th July, 1917, and go
        under orders of O.C. "E" Battalion.

(2)   Relief to commence at 9- 0 p.m. (i.e. time of leaving billets).

(3)   Stores, Kit, Mess Equipment, etc. will be ready for removal
        as under: -

                "D" Coy.   Coy. Hdqrs.   8-45 p.m.
                "B" "   SQUARE FARM.   9-45 p.m.

(4)   The Transport Officer will make the necessary arrangements
        for removal.

(5)   "B" Company will take over billets of "D" Company.
        Certificates will be exchanged that billets and lines have
        been taken over in a clean condition.

(6)   Relief complete will be signalled by B.A.B. Code.

                                (Sgd) J.H.BRADLEY, Lieut. & Adjt.,
                                        "H" Battalion.

                COPY No. 1   O.C.
                        2   O.C. "B" Coy.
                        3   O.C. "D" "
                        4   O.C. "E" Bn.
                        5   Transport Officer.
                        6   Lewis Gun Officer.
                        7   File.
                        8   War Diary.
                        9   "   "

SECRET.   RELIEF ORDER No.3.
          by Lieut-Colonel O.H.North. D.S.O., Commdg.
   In the Field.   "H" Battalion.   5th July, 1917.

APPENDIX IV

1. RELIEF.
   "H" Battalion will relieve "E" Battalion in L'EPINETTE SECTOR on the night of 10/11th July, 1917.

2. DISTRIBUTION.

COMPANY		SUB-SECTOR
"A"	Lieut. W. Ross.	Right.
"B"	Capt. J.H. Riley.	Right-Centre.
"C"	Major. T.L. Bailes.	Left-Centre.
"D"	Capt. J.E. Smitham.	Left.

3. TIMES OF RELIEF.
   "B" and "C" Companies will leave Billets 9.45 p.m. "A" Coy 10pm. "D" Company will arrange relief with O.C. Coy. "E" Battn. to be relieved, relief to be complete by 10 p.m.

4. ROUTE.
   "A" & "B" Coys.   BRICKSTACK LANE.
   "C" Company.   LUNATIC LANE.

5. LEWIS GUNS.
   Lewis Guns will move into Subsidiary Line on night of 9/10th July, 1917, leaving Billets at 9.45 p.m. Relief will be carried out at daybreak 10th July - Small parties at a time.

6. COMPLETION OF RELIEF.
   Relief complete will be signaled by B.A.B. Code.

7. MENS VALISES.
   All valises and spare kit, will be handed in to Q.M. Stores, at 7 p.m. July 10th, receipts being obtained.

8. BILLETS.
   Billets will left clean. One N.C.O. per Coy will be detailed to hand over to incoming Unit and will obtain certificate that billets have been handed over in a clean condition.

9. RESERVE S.A.A., GRENADES ETC.
   Bombing Officer will detail an N.C.O. to hand over Reserve S.A.A. Grenades etc, obtaining receipt in duplicate, one copy to be furnished to Battalion H.Q. by 9 a.m. 11th July.

10. RELIEF WILL BE SUBJECT TO POSTPONEMENT AT VERY SHORT NOTICE.

                                        (Sgd) J.H.BRADLEY. Lieut & Adjt.
                                                "H" Battalion.

   Copy No. 1. C.O.   Copy No. 8. T.O.
           2. 2nd in Command.   9. Q.M.
           3. O.C. "A" Coy.   10. O.C. Signals.
           4. "   "B" "   11. L.G. Officer.
           5. "   "C" "   12. War Diary.
           6. "   "D" "   13. "   "
           7. "E" Battalion.   14. File.

SECRET.

APPENDIX V

Copy No. 15.

RELIEF ORDER NO.4
by Lieut-Colonel. O.H. North, D.S.O.,
Commanding "H" Battalion.

14th July. 1917.

1. In accordance with Brigade Order No.18 dated 13th July.1917. "H" Battalion will be relieved by "E" Battalion on the night of 14/15th July. 1917.

2. Relief to commence at 9.30 p.m. (i.e. time of leaving billets).

3. Lewis Guns and personnel of "E" Battalion will move into Subsidiary Line on night of 14/15th July. 1917.
Relief will be carried out by daylight on 15th July in small parties at a time.
Lewis Guns of "H" Battalion will remain in Line until after 6p.m. on 15th July.

4. "A" Company on being relieved will go into Subsidiary Line and remain under Orders of O.C. "E" Battalion.

5. "B" Company will move out by BRICKSTACK LANE.
   "C"   "   "   "   "   " LUNATIC LANE.
   "D"   "   "   "   "   " BUTTERNE AVENUE.

   "B" Company will not commence to use BRICKSTACK LANE until C.T. is clear, approximately 10.30 p.m.

   All specialists (Signallers, Snipers, etc.) will move out with their respective Companies.
   Battn. H.Q. after being relieved will move out by BRICKSTACK LANE but will not enter C.T. before 10.45 p.m.

6. "H" Battalion less "A" Coy will take over Billets of "E" Battn. and go in Right Reserve.

7. All trench stores, logbooks, maps, defence and retaliation schemes etc., will be handed over on relief.
Receipts in duplicate will be obtained and one copy handed in to Battn. Orderly Room by 12 noon 15th July.

8. Lines will be handed over in a clean and sanitary condition.

9. When relieved, companies will move out independently, pace not to exceed two miles per hour.

10. Officers' kits, mess equipment etc., will be at respective Dumps by 10 p.m.
Medical equipment to be at SQUARE FARM at that time.
Os.C. Coys will each provide a loading party of 1 N.C.O. and 3 men.

11. When relieved, Companies and Specialists will advise Bn. H.Q. by Code.

(Sgd) J.H. BRADLEY. Lieut & Adjt.
"H" Battalion.

Copy No. 1. O.C.
         2. 2nd in Cd.
         3. O.C. "A" Coy.
         4. "   "B" "
         5. "   "C" "
         6. "   "D" "
         7. "E" Battn.
         8. O.C.Coy. "E" Battn.

Copy No. 9. L.G. Officer.
        10. O.C. Signals.
        11. M.O.
        12. Q.M.
        13. T.O.
        14. War Diary.
        15. "   "
        16. File.

APPENDIX. VI   9

RELIEF ORDER No. 3.
by Lieut-Colonel C.E.North.D.S.O.,Commanding,
In the Field.   "B" Battalion.

1. "B" Company will relieve "A" Company in Subsidiary Line at R SIXTY NORTH, on night 19/20th July, 1917, and go under Orders of O.C. "B" Battalion.

2. Relief to commence at 6.15 p.m. (i.e. time of leaving billets).

3. Stores, Kit, Mess equipment etc, will be ready for removal as under :-

   "B" Company. Roy.H.Q. 4.30 p.m.
   "A"   "   . SQUARE FARM. 4.0 p.m.

4. The Transport Officer will make the necessary arrangements for removal.

5. "A" Company will take over Billets of "B" Company. Certificates will be exchanged that Billets and lines have been taken over in a clean condition.

6. Relief complete will be signalled by B.A.B. Code.

                              (Sgd) J.R.SWAREY, Lieut.& Adjt.
                                       "B" Battalion.

        Copy No 1. C.O.
               2. O.C. "B" Company.
               3. "   "A"   "
               4. O.C. "D" Battn.
               5. Transport Officer.
               6. Lewis Gun Officer.
               7. File.
               8. War Diary.

SECRET.   APPENDIX   Copy No. 12

RELIEF ORDER NO. 6
by Lieut-Colonel O.H.North, D.S.O., Cmdg,
In the Field.   "H" Battalion.   22nd July, 1917.

---

1. **RELIEF.**
   two Coys. of "H" Battalion will relieve *two Coys. of* "E" Battalion in L'EPINETTE SECTOR on the night of 23rd/24th July, 1917.

2. **DISTRIBUTION.**

Company.	Sub-Sector.
"A" Lieut. H.S.Wilson.	Right.
"B" Capt. J.H.Riley.	Right-Centre.

3. **TIMES OF RELIEF.**
   "A" Company will leave Billets 9-15 p.m.
   "B" Company will arrange relief with O.C.Coy. "E" Battalion to be relieved, relief to be complete by 10 p.m.

4. **ROUTE.**
   "A" Company.   BRICKSTACK LANE.

5. **LEWIS GUNS.**
   Lewis Guns will move into Subsidiary Line on night of 23rd/24th July, 1917, leaving Billets at 10 p.m. Relief will be carried out at daybreak 24th July - small parties at a time.

6. **COMPLETION OF RELIEF.**
   Relief complete will be signalled by B.A.B. Code.

7. **MENS' VALISES.**
   All valises and spare kit will be handed in to Q.M.Stores at 7 p.m. 23rd July, receipts being obtained.

8. **MAGAZINES.**
   A minimum of 40 magazines per gun will be taken by relieving teams, and a similar number will be brought out by those relieved.

9. **BILLETS.**
   Billets will be left clean. One N.C.O. will be detailed to hand over to incoming unit and will obtain certificate that billets have been handed over in a clean condition.

10. **RESERVE S.A.A., GRENADES, ETC.**
    Bombing Officer will detail an N.C.O. to hand over Reserve S.A.A. Grenades etc., obtaining receipt in duplicate, one copy to be furnished to Btn. H.Q. by 9 a.m. 24th July.

(Sgd) J.H.BRADLEY,
Lieut & Adjutant,
"H" Battalion.

Copy No.		Copy No.	
1	C.O.	8	T.O.
2	2nd in Cd.	9	Q.M.
3	O.C. "A" Coy.	10	O.C. Signals.
4	"B"	11	L.G. Officer.
5	"C"	12	War Diary.
6	"D"	13	" "
7	"E" Battalion.	14	File.

APPENDIX VIII.

171st INFANTRY BRIGADE.

REPORT ON MINOR OPERATIONS CARRIED OUT IN L'EPINETTE SUB-SECTOR

on night of 25th/26th July, 1917.

by the 2/8th Bn. The King's (L'pool Regt) Lt-Col. O.H.North, D.S.O.
Commanding.

STRENGTH OF PARTY.	3 Officers; 122 Other Ranks.
POINT OF EXIT.	I.5.c. 80.90 - I.5.c.50.57.
POINT OF ENTRY.	I.5.d.27.59 - I.5.c.86.28.
TIME.	2 a.m.
OBJECT.	(a) Effect demonstration to assist Operations elsewhere. (b) Killing and capturing as many of the enemy as possible. (c) Capturing and destroying war material, demolising of Machine Gun and Minenwerfer emplacements.
NARRATIVE.	On the opening of the barrage, in consequence of the necessary bridges not being in position, the Raiding party was somewhat disorganised, and the majority of the party had not reached the jumping of place. This disorganisation resulted in the Assault Parties arriving at the enemy wire much behind on scheduled time. Here the O.C.Support Line Assault became a casualty, and which further hindered the execution of the operation. By this time the enemy had placed a barrage on his own front line which prevented an entrance.
ESTIMATED CASUALTIES.	1 Officer and 3 O.R. wounded.

(Sgd) O.H.NORTH Lt-Col.
Commanding,

26.7.17.

APPENDIX VIII

O.C.,
"H" Battalion.

....

The two officers in raid arrived at front line 12.15 a.m. Their duties were to mark point of assembly with luminous sign boards, to send of B.T. parties in sufficient time and assemble parties in N.M.L. by Zero minus 5.

On arrival in Front Line the bridges had not all arrived and did not all finally arrivae until 1-20 a.m. due apparently to carrying parties losing their way, and were not placed in position until 1.40 a.m. It was therefore impossible to send out B.T. parties sufficiently in advance to achieve their object, although every effort was made to do so, the parties starting out but were not able to reach their objective in time. The opening of our barrage 2½ mins. before zero contributed further to the failure of these parties. When barrage opened parties were not assembled according to plan owing to bridges not being in position. Difficulties were also experienced with bridges for enemy burrow ditch, some of these could not be found at the time and others had been dumped in our borrow ditch in such a position as to make the speedy handling of them impossible. Only one party on the right were able to get their bridge about half-way over.

Owing to parties not assembling as per programme the advance across N.M.L. was disorganised and delayed the rear parties losing touch the consequence being that the enemy barrage was well established on his own front line.

Under these circumstances the B.T. having failed, the bridges not being up and the enemy barrage heavy, the officers in charge of parties being deemed it inadvisable to proceed further with the few men who had been able to keep in touch and gave orders to withdraw, which was effected with very light casualties.

Officer in Charge left party (2nd Lieut. A.E.Anderson,M.C.) got through the enemy wire and was hit, but as he had so few men with him he sent the pre-arranged signal to officer in charge right party, that he had not got in to enemy line, in consequence of which officer in charge right party did not consider it advisable to proceed further and withdrew.

(Sgd) J.E.SMITHAM, Capt.
O.C.Raid.

26.7.1917.

SECRET.

APPENDIX IX
Copy No. 1.

RELIEF ORDER No. 7
by
Lieut-Colonel O.H.North, D.S.O., Cmdg.,
In the Field.   "H" Battalion.   26.7.1917.

----

1. RELIEF. Reference Brigade Order No. 20 dated 22.7.1917 "C" Coy. and "D" Coys. will relieve "C" and "D" Coys. of "E" Battn. in L'EPINETTE Sector on night of 27th/28th July, 1917.

2. DISTRIBUTION.   Company.   Sub-Sector.
                            "C"   Left-Centre.
                      Major T.L.Bailes.
                            "D"   Left.
                      Captain J.E.Smitham.

3. Times of Relief. "C" Coy. 9-15 p.m. Time of leaving billets.
                     "D" Coy. By arrangements with O.C. Coy. to be relieved.

4. ROUTE.   "C" Coy.   LUNATIC LANE.
   On being relieved Coys. will move out as under:-

                 "C" Coy. "E" Bn.   LUNATIC LANE.
                 "D" Coy. "E" Bn.   BUTERNE AVENUE.

5. LEWIS GUNS. Relief of Lewis Guns will take place at daybreak July 28th.

6. TRENCH STORES. Trench Stores, Log Books, Defence Schemes, etc. will be handed over on relief and receipts in duplicate obtained. One copy to be handed in to Bn. Orderly Room by 12 noon 28th July

7. LINES. Lines will be handed over in a clean condition and certificates to this effect obtained.

8. COMPLETION OF RELIEF. Relief Complete will be notified to Bn. H.Q. by B.A.B. Code.

                                         Lieut & Adjt.,
                                         "H" Battalion.

      Copy No. 1. C.O.   Copy No. 9. O.C. "D" Coy. "E" Bn.
              2.   2nd in Cde   10. O.C. Signals.
              3.   O.C. "A" Coy.   11. Transport Officer.
              4.   "B"   12. Lewis Gun Officer.
              5.   "C"   13. Quartermaster.
              6.   "D"   14. War Diary.
              7.   O.C. "E" Bn.   15   "   "
              8.   O.C. "C" Coy. "E" Bn.   16. File.

APPENDIX I

SPECIAL REPORT – "H" BN. – L'EPINETTE SECTOR.

30th JULY, 1917.

About 0-15 a.m. a party of about seven of enemy entered our trench at No. 8 Locality. Attention was first drawn to their presence by the firing of several rifle shots.

The bombers on Nos. 8 and 9 Posts at once proceeded to the spot but the enemy had retired. Lewis Gun fire was opened on to N.M.L.

One bomber of No. 9 post who had left previously to go to No. 8 post was killed.

The enemy had apparently taken advantage of the salient to obtain cover for his approach and return.

F. H. Bowring.
Major,
Commanding, "H" Battalion.

30.7.1917.

Appendix XI

H.Q.
171st Infantry Brigade.

....

At 2.30a.m. the enemy placed a Heavy Minnie Barrage on our Front Line over F Gap and Nos 5 & 6 Localities, and formed a box with Shrapnel & H.E. along Japan Avenue, Wollow Walk & Plank Avenue. Shrapnel & H.E. were also thrown over the Subsidiary Line between Port. Egal Avenue & Quality St.

The S.O.S. was sent up at 2.45a.m. The enemy barrage ceased at 3a.m. and the S.O.S. was stopped at 3.5a.m.

Very considerable damage was done to the front line, and communication with the front post was cut off.

Our casualties up to the time of writing are 15 wounded. 7 of the Battn. and 8 of "E" Battn.

                                               Major.
                                    Commdg. "H" Battalion.

31.7.17.

Appendix F

H.Q.
17 1st Infantry Brigade.

....

At 9.15p.m. a Heavy Minnie Barrage was placed on our Front Line over No 5 & 6 Localities. It was reported by two of the Sentries on No 8 Post that a number of the enemy were advancing towards our trench. Lewis Gun & Rifle fire was at once opened, and the N.C.O. in charge of the Post sent up the S.O.S. Signal which was at once taken up by the Trench Officer All quiet was signalled at 9.45p.m. Patrols were at once organised and search was made of N.M.L. but no trace of enemy could be found. Considerable damage was done to the Front Line.

Major.
Commdg. "H" Battalion.

31.7.17.

WAR DIARY or INTELLIGENCE SUMMARY

Army Form C. 2118

2/5 Liverpool Regt Vol 7

Place	Date	Hour	Summary of Events and Information	Remarks and references to Appendices
Estaminet Corner	Sept 1		Relieved by 2/5 L.R. in Cordonnerie Sector. Half Battalion move into Estaminet Hamencourt, Half remain in subsidiary line.	APPENDIX I
Hamencourt	2	9¾ pm	Move into reserve in Cordonnerie Sector. During day an unimportant amount of T.M.s were exchanged from the O.M.J. store which had been destroyed to five.	II
Rouge de Bout	3		Relief of 9th Hoylett Bath in the Bridoux-Moulière sector succeeded — a good change from Estaires.	III
	4		Nil	
	5			
	6			
	7			
Bridoux	8		Relieved by 2/5 H.L.R. (Plus two coys.) Plus two coys of H.Q. of L.R.	IV
Rouge de Bout	9		Reserve in retrenchment line at Haute Epinette	V
	16	2 p.m.	Relieve 2/5 South L.L.R. in Cordonnerie Sector.	VI
Cordonnerie	17/23		Quiet line. Casualties only 4 wounded. Drafts received 61 O.R. 29/8/15 17 O.R. 27/8/15	VII
	24		Relieved by 1/5 B. Lynx Regt. in CORDONNERIE Sector and returned to Billets at ROUGE DE BOUT.	
Rouge de Bout	25/31		Draft of 40 O.R. reported from 24 Inf. Base Depot. 26 O.R. Browning ready.	7

SECRET.   Appendix I Copy No. 12.
                              RELIEF ORDER NO.
                        by Major E.S.Hoare MC, Commdg.,
              In the Field, "D" Battalion, 1st August, 1918.
              ----

1.   In accordance with 171st Bde. Order No.   , the 2/4th
        L.N.L.R. will relieve the 1/4th Bn. D.L.I. in NIEPPE TOWN
        SECTOR on the night of August 1st/2nd.

2.   Each Company will be relieved by the corresponding Coy. of the
        2/4th L.N.L.R.

3.   "A" and "B" Coys. on relief will proceed to Subsidiary Line.
        "C" and "D" Coys. will proceed to billets in ARMENTIERES,
        as under:-
                "C" Coy.   RUE DE LA PAIX.
                "D" "   CONVENT OF LITTLE SISTERS OF THE POOR.
        These two Coys. will move out via BRICKSTOCK LANE.
        O.C. Coys. will ascertain that this trench is clear before
        using same.

4.   Lewis Guns of all Coys. will proceed to Subsidiary Line
        on relief.

5.   Os.C. respective Specialist Sections will arrange relief
        with O.C. respective sections of relieving unit, and report
        to Bn. H.Q. when relieved.

6.   Relief Complete will be signalled by S.O.S.Code.

7.   (i) All Trench Stores, Log Books, Maps, Defence Schemes,
        and necessary records will be handed over on relief.
        Receipts will be obtained, one copy to be handed in to Bn.
        H.Q.
        (ii) All telescopes, patrol suits, Very Lights, periscopes,
        and any other articles on charge of this Unit will be
        brought out of the line.
                                                 and sanitary
8.   Lines will be handed over in a clean/condition.
        A receipt to this effect will be obtained by each Company.

9.   Officers' kit, Coy. Stores etc. to be at SQUARE FARM at
        Bn. H.Q.; also Medical Equipment.
        Os.C. "C" and "D" Coys. will each provide a loading party
        of 1 N.C.O. and 2 men.

10.   Transport Officer will arrange to move baggage of "C" and
        "D" Coys. and kits and to supply rations to billets
        occupied by them in ARMENTIERES.
        He will also arrange to supply rations to "A" and "B" Coys.
        in Subsidiary Line.

11.   Os.C. "C" and "D" Coys. will arrange for rations of Lewis
        Gunners to be sent to Subsidiary Line.

                                            E J Woodcock
                                            2nd Lieut., A/Adjt.,
                                            "D" Battalion.

        Copy No.1 O.C.   Copy No. 8 L.G.Officer.
                2 T/Major.   9 O.C.Signals.
                3 O.C."A" Coy.   10 2/4th L.N.L.R.
                4   " "B" "   11 M.O.
                5   " "C" "   12 War Diary.
                6   " "D" "   13   "   "
                7 T.O.   14 File.

SECRET.   *Appendix II*   Copy No. 13

W. Diary

ORDERS
by Major F.H.Bowring, Cmdg.,
In the Field.   "H" Battn.   2nd Aug.1917.
----

1. In accordance with Brigade Order No. 23, the Battalion will move into Brigade Reserve in the CORDONERIE SECTOR on the night of 2/3rd August, 1917.
   The Subsidiary Line and Defence will be under command of O.C. 2/8th K.L.R.

2. Billeting Parties of 1 N.C.O. and 2 men per Company will parade under 2nd Lieut. W.Redding at Battn. H.Q. (Convent) at 9 a.m. 2/8/17 and will report to H.Q. 170th Bde - FLEURBAIX H.20.d.6.6. at 12 noon, where they will be met by guides arranged by Staff Captain, 170 Brigade.

3. "C" and "D" Coys. will leave billets immediately on arrival of 2/4th L.N.L.Regt. and will proceed to Billets at ROUGE DE BOUT.H.8.a.03.66. Billets will be handed over in a clean condition, receipts to this effect being obtained.

4. "A" and "B" Coys. on relief will proceed to billets at ROUGE DE BOUT. Route-from trenches to Railway Crossing H.8.a.03.96 ERQUINGHEM - ARMENTIERES ROAD. This is left to discretion of Company Commanders.

5. March Formations. From Railway Crossing H.8.a.03.96 to Factory ERQUINGHEM - half Platoons in file at 50 paces interval. From Factory to Billets Companies will march in column of route., 50 paces interval between platoons.

6. Lewis Guns/ of "A" and "B" Coys. will march with their respective Coys.
   Lewis Guns of "C" and "D" Coys. will move out under orders of Lewis Gun Officer.

7. Route to be followed by all parties from Railway Crossing H.8.a.03.96 ERQUINGHEM-ARMENTIERES ROAD to FORT ROMPU - left - FLEURBAIX ROAD -Right-after passing Level Crossing along RUE PATTAILLE and RUE QUESNOY to Billets.

8. Guides will meet Coys. at 12 midnight at junction of roads G.2.d.1.0.05. RUE QUESNOY - RUE DE BRUGES.

9. O.C."B" Coy. will obtain from O.C. 2/5th L.N.L.Regt. all Very Pistols lent on night of 1st/2nd Aug:.

10. Transport Officer will make necessary arrangements. ~~for Transport.~~

11. Loading Parties of 1 N.C.O. and 3 men will be detailed by Os.C.Coys.

12. Stores of "C" and "D" Coys. and H.Q. will be ready to move at 8 p.m.
    "A" and "B" Coys. at SQUARE FARM at 9 p.m.

(Sgd) E.J.WOODCOCK, 2/Lt. & Actg Adjt.,
"H" Battalion.

Copy No.		Copy No.	
1.	C.O.	8	T.O.
2.	H.Q.	9.	S.O.
3.	O.C."A"Coy.	10.	M.O.
4.	"B"	11.	2/4 L.N.L.R.
5.	"C"	12.	War Diary.
6.	"D"	13.	" "
7.	L.G.Officer.	14.	File.

Ref: Map. Sheet 36 Ed: 6
1/40,000.

SECRET.   Appendix III   Copy No. 12

Ref: Map Sheet 36   RELIEF ORDER NO. 2
Sd: 6.1/40,000.   by Major F.H.Bowring, Commanding,
   Relief   In the Field.   "H" Bn.   3rd Aug, 1917.
   ───

1.   2/8th (Irish) Bn. K.L.R. will relieve the 8th Bn. Norfolk Regt.
     in CORDONNERIE SECTOR on the night of 3rd/4th August, 1917.

2.   The distribution of Coys. is as follows:-
                                              Coy. of 8th Norfolks
     Coy.   Sub-Sector.   being relieved.
     ─────   ──────────   ──────────────────
     "A"   Right.   "D"
     CAPT A.C.WRIGHT ~~Lt. H.G.Wilson.~~
     "B"   Centre.   "C"
     Capt. J.H.Pilley.
     "D"   Left.   "A"
     2nd Lt. W.S.Lofthouse.
     "C"   Reserve.   "B"
     Major T.L.Bailes.

3.   "A" and "D" Coys. will arrange to leave billets in time to
     arrive at Bn. Hdqrs G.36.d.9.7. at 8-30 p.m.
     "B" and "C" Coys. will arrange to leave billets in time to
     arrive at Bn. Hdqrs G.36.d.9.7. at 8-45 p.m.
     Here Coys. will be met at the times stated by 4 guides per
     Coy. of unit being relieved.

4.   From Bn. Hdqrs Coys. will move by platoons in single file at
     200 yards distance.
     This order must be strictly adhered to.

5.   Os.C. respective Specialist Sections will arrange relief with
     Os.C. respective sections of unit being relieved, and report
     to Bn. Hdqrs when relieved.

6.   Relief Complete will be signalled by B.A.B. Code.

7.   A list of all Trench Stores taken over will be sent to Bn. Hdqrs
     by 6 p.m. on 4.8.17.

8.   Billets will be handed over clean, and handing over certificates
     forwarded to Bn. Hdqrs by 12 noon 4.8.17.

9.   Transport Officer will make necessary arrangements regarding
     transport.

10. Parties to load, accompany, and unload wagons will be detailed
     by Os.C. Coys.

11. All Stores etc. to be ready for loading by 7 p.m.

                                    (Sgd) E.J. WOODCOCK 2/Lieut.
                                                 and Actg Adjt.,
                                             "H" Battalion.

     Copy No. 1   C.O.   Copy No. 8.   Transport Officer.
            2.   Bombing Officer.   9.   Signal Officer.
            3.   O.C. "A" Coy.   10.   Medical Officer.
            4.   "B"   11.   8th Norfolk Regt.
            5.   "C"   12.   War Diary.
            6.   "D"   13.   "
            7.   Lewis Gun Officer.   14.   File.

SECRET.   Appendix IV   Copy No. 19

RELIEF ORDER NO. 10
by Major F.H.BOWRING, Commanding,
2nd Line 8th (Irish) Bn. Liverpool Regiment.   7.8.1917.

----

1. In accordance with Brigade Order No. 25, the 2/8th (Irish) Bn. Liverpool Regiment will be relieved by 2 Coys. of 2/5th K.L.R. and 2 Coys. of 2/6th K.L.R. in the COMDONNERIE SECTOR on the night of 8th/9th August, 1917, and will proceed to Billets at ROUGE DE BOUT.

2. Os.C.Coys. will detail 1 N.C.O. and 6 men to take over billets as occupied by this Battalion on night of 2nd/3rd August, 1917.

3. 3 men from A & B Coys will be detailed to report at Bn. H.Q. of 2/5th K.L.R. ROUGE DE BOUT at 8 p.m. on the 8th August to act as guides to incoming unit. 3 men from C & D Coys will report at this Bn. H.Q. at 8 p.m.

4. On relief one platoon per Company will proceed to Subsidiary Line as under:-
   1 Platoon of "A" Coy.   CHARRED POST.
   1   "   " "B" "   WINDY POST.
   1   "   " "C" "   (2 Sections   WINTERNIGHT'S POST.
                        (2   "   JUNCTION POST.
   1   "   " "D" "   CROIX BLANCHE.

5. O.C. 2/5th K.L.R. will detail 1 guide per platoon for Subsidiary Line.
   Guides for CHARRED POST and WINDY POST will meet platoons at entrance to V.C.EXTENSION - RUE DELVAS.
   Guides for WINTERNIGHT'S POST, JUNCTION POST, and CROIX BLANCHE, will meet platoons at junction of RUE BRASSIERES and RUE PETILLION.

6. Os.C.Specialists Sections will arrange reliefs with Os.C. respective Specialists Sections of 2/5th K.L.R.

7. Lines will be handed over in a clean condition and receipts to that effect obtained, one copy to be handed in to Bn. H.Q. by 9 a.m. 9.8.17.

8. Officers' Kit, Coy. Stores, Medical Equipment, etc. will be at respective dumps ready for loading by 8 p.m.

9. Relief Complete will be signalled by B.A.B.Code.

10. Transport Officer will make necessary arrangements regarding transport.

11. Os.C.Coys. will each detail 1 man to guide transport to billets.

12. A List of all Trench Stores handed over will be handed in to Bn. H.Q. by 12 noon 9.8.17.

                                        (Sgd) E.J.WOODCOCK, 2/Lt. &
                                                        Actg Adjt.,
                                        2/8th (Irish) Bn. Liverpool Regiment.

Copy No. 1   C.O.   Copy No. 8 2/5th K.L.R.
        2   2/5th K.L.R.   9 Signal Officer.
        3   O.C. "A" Coy.   10 Medical Officer.
        4   "B" "   11 Transport Officer.
        5   "C" "   12 War Diary.
        6   "D" "   13   "   "
        7   Lewis Gun Officer.   14 File.

SECRET.   1/8th (Irish) Bn. K.L.R.   Appendix V
                           INSTRUCTION NO. 1.
                Reference:- ....
                     FLEURBAIX   N.W.3.   do.

1. It is possible that the enemy may start a limited offensive against part of this Corps Front in order to divert attention from other parts of his line or for purely political reasons. The most likely place to be attacked which would affect this Brigade is NEUVE CHAPELLE.

2. In the event of the enemy gaining a temporary success, it may be necessary to move the Res. Bn. in the POUTILLERIE SECTOR to the the threatened position.

3. (a) The Bn. will be drawn up (50 yds between Platoons) on the RUE DU BIACHE (N.20.d., N.21.A.) at Zero Hour. Head of column at N.20.d.90.90.

(b) Subsidiary Line garrisons will join their Unit when ordered to do so by Brigade H.Qrs. They will be relieved by Platoons from the Bn. in Reserve, GONNEHEM SECTOR. If the matter is of extreme urgency they will be required to move before their reliefs arrive.

4. (a) Motor lorries will be provided for the conveyance of troops. These will report at FLEURBAIX on the RUE DE BIACHE, and will convey troops as far as HARROW ROAD (N.20) where they will be met by guides and conducted to their respective positions.

(b) If motor lorries are not available, troops will proceed on foot by forced march.

5. (a) Troops will be equipped in accordance with S.S.135,XXXI,para. 4, but the following will not be carried:- Packs. Cap Comforters. Cardigan Jackets. Aeroplane Flares. Sandbags. Picks and Shovels. S.O.S. Rockets and Wire-Cutters.

(b) Bombers and Grenadiers will carry 10 bombs per man, either in waistcoats or canvas buckets. Rifle Grenadiers will carry 5 rods and 5 blank cartridges each, in addition to the above.
Special attention is directed to Sub-paras. 6 and 7 of paras. XXXI (Hand Grenades and Ammunition).

(c) In addition, one box of S.A.A. will be carried in each lorry. this will be provided by Left Res. Bn.

6. It may be found that the Left Reserve Bn. is incapable of rapid assembly, owing to the absence of Platoons on Working Parties, in which case the Right Reserve Bn. will be called upon to supply its Emergency Company to proceed with the Emergency Company of the Left Reserve Bn. in advance of the main body. This Company will parade on the RUE DE BIACHE N.20.d. as ordered above.

7. The Emergency Coy. of this Bn. will be detailed from time to time in Bn. Orders, and will consist of One Complete Coy. the Platoon of this Coy. in the Subsidiary Line being relieved by an Emergency Platoon of another Coy. which will also be detailed. They will also be ready to move within one hour of the order being issued.

    Programmes
8. Training will not be altered on account of the possibility of this move, until orders are received to do so.

9. Troops will carry unexpended portion of the day's rations. Rations for the following day will be issued under arrangements to be made by the S.S.O. 57th Division.

10. Packs will be stored at Coy. H.Q. and a suitable Guard left. The place will be reported to Bn. H.Q. on departure of the Coys.

11. Supplies of Bombs and Rifle Grenades will be drawn by the Emergency Coy. from Reserve G.30.d.2.7. ROUGE DE VOUT with the exception of the Platoon in the Subsidiary Line; these will be drawn from Platoon Store.

12. ACKNOWLEDGE.
                                        E.J.Woodcock
                                        Lt. & A/cig Adjt.,
                                        8/8th (Irish) Bn. K.L.R.
4.6.17.

COPY NO. 1.   171st Infantry Brigade.
      2.   O.C. "A" Coy.
      3.   "B"
      4.   "C"
      5.   "D"
      6.   Commanding Officer.
      7.   War Diary.
      8.   "   "
      9.   File.
     10.   "

SECRET. *Appendix VI* Copy No. 13

RELIEF ORDER NO. 11
by Major F.H.Bowring, Commanding,
2nd Line 8th (Irish) Bn. Liverpool Regiment.   15.8.17.

Ref: Map Sheet 36 S.W. 1/40,000.

1. In accordance with Bde. Order No. 37, 2/8th K.L.R. will relieve 2/5th Bn. K.L.R. in CORDONNERIE SECTOR during afternoon of August 16th.

2. Distribution of Coys.

Company		Sub-Sector
"A" Captain H.C.Wright.		Right.
"B" Captain J.N.L.Bryan.		Centre.
"C" Captain Sir A.W.F.Bagge, Bt.		Left.
"D" Captain J.E.Smitham.		Reserve.

3. Relief will commence at 2 p.m.

4. Coys. will pass Bn. H.Q. and proceed by routes as below at times stated.
   - "A" RUE DELVAS and V.C. AVENUE.   2-30 p.m.
   - "B"   DO.   and CELLAR FARM AVENUE.   3-30 p.m.
   - "C" RUE DE BIACHE, DEVON AVENUE.   3 p.m.
   - "D" RUE DELVAS, RUE DE BOIS.   4 p.m.

5. Coys. will move by platoons at 200 yards distance.

6. Lewis Guns will precede Coys. and will pass Bn. H.Q. at 2 p.m.

7. 2nd Lt. J.A.FREE, M.C. will report to Left Coy. H.Q. of Right Bn. as Liason Officer and remain there during tour. O.C. "A" Coy. will detail 1 N.C.O. and 1 O.R. to report to left front line post of Right Bn. where they will remain during tour.

8. List of Trench Stores taken over will be sent to Bn. H.Q. by 9 a.m. August 17th.

9. Completion of Relief will be reported by wire "RATIONS REQUIRED".

10. Valises, spare kit, &c. will be handed in to Q.M.Stores at 12 noon.

11. O.C.Coys. will each detail party to remain with stores in billets, this party to load and accompany wagons.

12. Billets will be left in a clean condition, and certificate obtained to this effect.

(Sgd) J.H.BRADLEY, Lt. & Adjt.,
2nd Line 8th (Irish) Bn. Liverpool Regiment.

Copy No.		Copy No.	
1	Comdg Officer.	8	Q.M.
2	O.C."A" Coy.	9.	T.O.
3	"B"	10.	S.O.
4	"C"	11	M.O.
5	"D"	12	2/5th K.L.R.
6	L.G.O.	13	War Diary.
7	File.	14.	" "

RELIEF ORDER No 12.   Copy No. 13.
by Major F.H.Bowring, Commanding,
2nd Line 8th (Irish) Bn. K.L.R.

1. In accordance with 171st Brigade Order No 29, 2/8th (Irish) K.L.R. will be relieved by 2/5th K.L.R. in the CORDONNERIE SECTOR during the afternoon of August 24th, 1917.

2. Relief will commence at 2p.m.

3. On relief 2/8th(Irish)K.L.R. will withdraw into Brigade Reserve at ROUGE DE BOUT. Companies will occupy billets as on August 7th.

    1 Platoon "A"Coy. to occupy CHARRED POST.
    1   "   "B" "   "   WINDY POST.
    1   "   "C" "   "   WINTERS NIGHT & JUNCTION POSTS.
    1   "   "D" "   "   CROIX BLANCHE.

4. (i) All Trench Stores, Log Books, Maps, Defence Schemes etc will be handed over on relief, receipts being obtained in duplicate, one copy to be forwarded to Battalion H.Q. by 9a.m. August 25th. PROMPT.

   (ii) 1½" Very Pistols will be handed over to incoming Unit.

5. Lines will be handed over in a clean and sanitary condition, certificates being obtained to this effect.

6. All Coy. Stores, Kit etc will be stacked at Coy. Dumps. O.C. Companies will each detail a loading party to remain with stores.

7. Companies when relieved will move out independently by half platoons, 100 Yards distance.
    Complete
8. Relief will be signalled "LONDON".

                                    Capt & Adjt.
                        2/8th (Irish) Bn. K.L.R.

Copy No 1. C.O.   Copy No. 8. Q.M.
     2. O.C."A" Coy.   9. T.O.
     3.   "B"   10. S.O.
     4.   "C"   11. M.O.
     5.   "D"   12. 2/5th. K.L.R.
     6. L.G.O.   13. War Diary.
     7. File.   14. " "

Headquarters,
57th Division.

....

Herewith War Diary for month of September, 1917, with Appendices thereto.

　　　　　　　　　　　P.H.Nott
　　　　　　　　　　　　　　　　Lieut-Colonel,
Commanding 2nd Line 8th (Irish) Bn. Liverpool Regt.

In the Field.
30.9.1917.

Army Form C. 2118.

WAR DIARY
or
INTELLIGENCE SUMMARY.
(Erase heading not required.)

Instructions regarding War Diaries and Intelligence Summaries are contained in F. S. Regs., Part II. and the Staff Manual respectively. Title pages will be prepared in manuscript.

Place	Date	Hour	Summary of Events and Information	Remarks and references to Appendices
Longues Sect	1/9/17	-	Relief 23rd Bn K.L.R. on Eastward Sector Front Line 36-	Appendix I
			O.R. 4st	
Fauquissart	9/9/17		Relieved in 4th Bn K.L.R. 23rd O.R. Dept 4 gun	II
	16/9/17		" Bn Relief Relieved Bn in Line from Rue du Bacquerot	III
			2 Royal Regiment (Reserve)	
February	19/9/17		14th " in Reserve to Fauquissart	IV
Fauquissart	20/9/17		Battalion HQ Red Butes - Fortes.	V
Fortes	24/9/17		Programme of Training for the week. Ordinary Sun.	VI
			Ordinary training to Battalion allotted for Sub.	
			Nos. of ranks Dance Bar. To Battalion Line for Sun.	VII
-	29/9/17		work	
	26/9/17		Battalion Strength. Offrs 40 O.R. Rank 932	

SECRET.   RELIEF ORDER No 13.   Copy No. 13.
          by Major. F.H.Bowring, Commanding,
               2nd Line 8th(Irish)Bn.K.L.R.

APPENDIX T

1. In accordance with Bde. Order No 31, 2/8th K.L.R. will relieve 2/5th K.L.R. in CORDONNERIE SECTOR during afternoon of Sept.1st.

2. Distribution of Coys.

   Company.   Sub-Sector.
     "D"
   Capt. J.E.Smitham.   Right.
     "B"
   Capt. J.H.Riley.   Centre.
     "C"
   Major. T.L.Bailes.   Left.
     "A"
   Capt. H.C. Wright.   Reserve.

3. Relief will commence at 2p.m.

4. Companies will pass Battn. H.Q. and proceed by routes as below at times stated.
   "C" RUE DI BIACHE, DEVON AVENUE.   2.30p.m.
   "D" RUE DELVAS and V.C. AVENUE.   3.0p.m.
   "B"   do   " CELLAR FARM AV.   3.30p.m.
   "A"   do   " RUE DE BOIS.   4p.m.

5. Coys will move by Platoons at 200 yards distance.

6. Lewis Guns will precede Coys. and will pass Battn. H.Q. at 2p.m.

7. O.C. "A" Coy will detail an Officer to report to Right Battn. as Liason Officer, to remain there during tour.

8. List of Trench Stores taken over will be sent to Battn. H.Q. by 9a.m. Sept. 2nd. 1917.

9. Completion of Relief will be reported by wire "STORES REQUIRED".

10. O.C. Coys will each detail a party to remain with stores in billets, this party to load and accompany wagons.

11. Billets will be left clean in a clean condition, and certificate obtained to this effect.

                              (Capt & Adjt.
                              2/8th (Irish) BN. K.L.R.

   Copy No 1. C.O.   Copy No 8. Q.M.
          2. O.C."A" Coy.   9. T.O.
          3. "   "B" "   10. S.O.
          4. "   "C" "   11. M.O.
          5. "   "D" "   12. 2/5th. K.L.R.
          6. L.G.O.   13. War Diary.
          7. File.   14. "   "

SECRET.   RELIEF ORDER No 16.   Copy No. 13.
          by Major F.H. Bowring. Comndg.
          2nd Line 8th (Irish) Bn. K.L.R.
----

1. In accordance with 171st Brigade Order No 31, 2/8th (Irish) K.L.R. will be relieved by 2/5th K.L.R. in the CORDONNERIE SECTOR during the afternoon of September 9th 1917.

2. Relief will commence 2p.m.

3. On relief 2/8th (Irish) Bn. K.L.R. will withdraw into Brigade Reserve at ROUGE DE BOUT. Companies will occupy billets as on Sept. 1st.

    1 Platoon "A" Coy. to occupy CHARRED POST.
    1   "   "B" "   "   "   WIDOW POST.
    1   "   "C" "   "   "   WINTERS RIGHT & JUNCTION POSTS.
    1   "   "D" "   "   "   CROIX BLANCHE.

   One N.C.O. per Platoon will be detailed to take over stores at Strong Post at 2p.m.

4. (i) All Trench Stores, Log Books, Maps, Defence Schemes etc will be handed over on relief, receipts being obtained in duplicate, one copy to be forwarded to Battn. H.Q. by 8a.m. Sept. 10th.

   (ii) 10" Very Pistols will be handed to incoming Unit.

5. Lines will be handed over in a clean and sanitary condition, certificates being obtained to this effect.

6. All Coy. Stores, Kit etc will be stacked at Coy. Dumps. O.C. Coys will detail a loading party to remain with stores.

7. Coys when relieved will move out independently by half platoons 100 yards distance.

8. Relief complete will be signalled "WHISKEY"

                                            [signature]
                                            Capt & Adjt.
                                            2/8th. (Irish) Bn. K.L.R.

   Copy No 1. C.O.   Copy No 8. Q.M.
        " 2. O.C. "A" Coy.   " 9. T.O.
        " 3. "   "B" "   " 10. S.O.
        " 4. "   "C" "   " 11. M.O.
        " 5. "   "D" "   " 12. 2/5th K.L.R.
        " 6. L.G.O.   " 13. War Diary.
        " 7. File.   " 14. "   "

APPENDIX III
Copy No. 17.

RELIEF ORDER NO. 18
by Lieut-Col. O.H.North, D.S.O., Cmdg.,
2nd Line 8th (Irish) Bn. Liverpool Regiment.
16th Sept. 1917.

RELIEF. 1. (a) 14th Bn. Welsh Regiment will relieve 2nd Line 8th
(Irish) Bn. Liverpool Regiment in Brigade Right Reserve,
FLEURBAIX Sector, on September 16th, 1917.
(b) On relief, 2nd Line 8th (Irish) Bn. Liverpool Regt.
will proceed by march route to billets at NEUF BERQUIN.

DISPOSITION 2. Coys. of incoming unit will relieve corresponding Coys.
OF COYS. viz:- "A" Coy. 14th Welsh Regt. will relieve "A" Coy.
2/8th (Irish) Bn. K.L.R. in billets and subsidiary line.

GUIDES. 3. (a) 2 Guides per Coy., one each from Transport and Bn.
Hdqrs. will parade at Bn. Headquarters at 9 a.m. under
2nd Lieut. J.M.Thornton and proceed to Road Junction
RUE DE LA LYS G.27.d.3.8. where incoming Unit will be
met at 11 a.m.
(b) 1 Guide per Platoon in Subsidiary Line will parade
at Bn. Hdqrs. at 11-30 a.m. and conduct their respective
incoming Platoon to Subsidiary Line.

TRENCH & 4. All Trench and Area Stores will be handed over to
AREA STORES. incoming Unit, receipts in TRIPLICATE being forwarded
to Bn. Hdqrs. by 9 P.M. Septr. 16th, 1917.

ON COMPLE- 5. (1) On Completion of Relief in Billets.
TION OF (a) Coys. (less 1 Platoon in Subsidiary Line) will march
RELIEF. independently to LE NOUVEAU MONDE, head of column to
rest on road RUE DE LA LYS by Church.
(b) Battalion (less 1 Platoon per Company) will proceed thence
by March Route to NEUF BERQUIN.
Route:- RUE DE LA LYS, ESTAIRES.
(2) On Completion of Relief in Subsidiary Line.
(a) Platoons will march independently to "A" Coy. Billet
where they will rendezvous.
Route:- Bn. Hdqrs, RUE DES FIEFS, Road left-handed,
Road Right-handed.
(b) Thence the four Platoons will proceed under Captain
W.Ross by March Route to NEUF BERQUIN.
Route:- RUE DE LA LYS, ESTAIRES.

MARCH 6. An interval of 100 yards will be maintained between Platoons
DISCIPLINE. on the march while on the South-East side of the LAVENTIE-
ERQUINGHEM Railway.

BILLETS, 7. Billets and Subsidiary Line will be handed over in a clean
LINES AC. condition, certificates being obtained to this effect.

OFFICERS' 8. Officers' Kits will be packed ready for Transport by 8 a.m.
KITS. 16.9.17.

COOKERS. 9. Cookers will be ready for removal at 1 P.M.

Captain & Adjutant,
2nd Line 8th (Irish) Bn. K. L. R.

Copy No. 1 O.C.   Copy No. 7 O.C. WINDY POST.   Copy No. 13 L.G.O.
        2 2nd in Cd.   8   "   JUNCTION   "   14 Q.M.
        3 O.C. "A" Coy.   9   "   CHAPPED   "   15 T.O.
        4   "   "B" "   10   "   CROIX BLANCHE P.   16 War Diary.
        5   "   "C" "   11   "   ──────────── M.O. 17
        6   "   "D" "   12   "   Signals.   18 File.

SECRET.   APPENDIX IV   COPY NO. 13
OPERATION ORDER NO.16
by Lieut-Col. O.H.North, D.S.O., Cmdg.,
In the Field.   "H" Battn.   17.9.1917.

MOVE.   (1) In accordance with Bde. Order No. 34 dated 17.9.17 the
                    3/8th (Irish) Bn. K.L.R. will move from ROBERMETZ to
                    CANTRAINNE on Tuesday September 18th.

ROUTE.   (2) MERVILLE, road junction Q.3.b.3.5. CALONNE sur la Lys,
                    ROBECQ, l'ECLEME.

BILLETING   (3) A Billeting Party of 1 N.C.O. per Coy. and 1 N.C.O. Bn. Hdqrs
PARTY.   will parade at Battn. Hdqrs at 6 a.m. with cycles under
                    Captain W.E.Jones, and proceed to BUSNES. This party will
                    report to Staff Captain at 8 a.m. at BUSNES CHURCH.

PARADE.   (4) The Battalion will parade ready to move at 8-45 a.m. at
                    junction K.29.b.91.50, as under:-
                    Signallers, "B" & "A" Coys. and Transport on road ROBERMETZ -
                    MERVILLE.
                    "C" & "D" Coys. on road College - MERVILLE.
                    Head of Column in each case to be at K.29.b.91.50.

ORDER OF   (5)   Signallers.
MARCH.   "B" Company.
                               "C"   "
                               BAND.
                               "D" Company.
                               "A"   "

SYNCHRONIS-   Signalling Officer will send watch to be synchronised by
ATION OF   (6) Brigade Signalling Officer, LA GORGUE, at 6-30 a.m.
WATCHES.   Watches of Os.C.Coys. will be synchronised at Bn. Hdqrs.
                    7-30 a.m.

OFFICERS'   (7) Officers' Kits will be stacked at <u>Company Headquarters</u>
KITS.   by 7-30 a.m., <u>prompt</u>.

COOKERS.   (8) Cookers will be ready for removal at 7-45 a.m.

BILLETS.   (9) Billets will be left clean.

                                      (Sgd) J.H.BRADLEY, Captain & Adjt.,
                                            "H" Battalion.

            COPY NO. 1 O.C.   COPY NO. 8 M.O.
                     2. 2nd in Cd.   9 L.G.O.
                     3. O.C. "A" Coy.   10 Q.M.
                     4.   "B"   11 T.O.
                     5.   "C"   12 War Diary.
                     6.   "D"   13   "   "
                     7. O.C. Signals.   14. File.

SECRET. APPENDIX IV Copy No. 12

OPERATION ORDER No. 17
by Lieut.-Colonel O.H. North, D.S.O., Commdg.
In the Field.   "H" Battalion.   18.9.1917.

Move.	1.	In accordance with Bde Order No. 35, dated 18.9.17, "H" Battalion will move from CANTRAINNE to FONTES on Wednesday, 19.9.1917.
Route.	2.	U.11.a.15.30 – BOURECQ – St. HILAIRE – NORRENT FONTES.
Billeting Party.	3.	A Billeting Party of 1 N.C.O. per Coy. and will parade at Battn. H.Q. at 8 a.m. with cycles under Capt. W.E. Jones and will report to Staff Captain at 9 a.m. at T.6.c.1.1.
Parade.	4.	The Battalion will parade ready to move at 8.50 a.m. Head of column to be at U.12.b.3.9.
Dress, Cooks.	5.	Cooks will march in equipment, not in overalls.
Order of March.	6.	Signallers. "C" Coy. "D" " BAND. "A" Coy. "B" "
Officers' Kits.	7.	Officers' Kits will be stacked at Coy. H.Q. ready for collection at 7.30 a.m. prompt.
Cookers.	8.	Cookers will be ready for removal at 7.45 a.m.
Billets.	9.	Billets will be left clean.
Marching Out State.	10.	Marching Out State will handed to Adjt. at rendezvous 8.30 a.m.
Returns.	11.	(a) Certificate that payment for Mess Room has been made will be handed to Adjt. at Rendezvous. (b) Within one hour of arrival at FONTES Os. C. Coys. will render return of men who have fallen out on the march, each day to be shewn separately.
Saluting.	12.	When on the march, men on being called to attention will carry rifle slung on right shoulder, sling to the front.

Capt. and Adjutant,
"H" Battalion.

Copy No. 1.- O.C.   8. M.O.
        2   2nd in Cd.   9 L.G.O.
        3   O.C. "A"   10 Q.M.
        4   "   "B"   11 T.D.
        5   "   "C"   12 War Diary.
        6   "   "D"   13   "
        7   Signals Offr. 14 File.

Headquarters,
...st Infantry Brigade.

APPENDIX VI

TRAINING PROGRAMME.

FIRST WEEK.

1st Day.	8.30 – 9.30 a.m.	Physical and Bayonet Fighting.
	9.30 – 11.30 a.m.	Squad Drill.
	11.30 – 12.30 p.m.	Musketry.
2nd Day.	do.	do.
3rd Day.	8.30 – 9.30 a.m.	Physical and Bayonet Fighting.
	9.30 – 10.30 a.m.	Arms Drill.
	10.30 – 11.30 a.m.	Squad Drill.
	11.30 – 12.30 p.m.	Musketry.
4th Day.	8.30 – 9.30 a.m.	Physical and Bayonet Fighting.
	9.30 – 10. 0 a.m.	Platoon Drill.
	10. 0 – 10.30 a.m.	Gas Drill.
	10.30 – 11. 0 a.m.	Musketry.
	11. 0 – 12.30 p.m.	Sections in use of own weapons.
5th Day.	do.	do.
6th Day.	do.	do.

Organised Games every afternoon, 2 p.m. to 4.30 p.m.
Lectures, 6 p.m. to 6.30 p.m. for Section Commanders.
Signallers commence training "Forward Intercommunication &c. in Battle" after 3rd day.

SECOND WEEK.

1st Day.	8.30 – 9.30 a.m.	Physical and Bayonet Fighting.
	9.30 – 12. 0 noon.	Musketry.
	12. 0 – 12.30 p.m.	Company Drill.
2nd Day.	8.30 – 12.30 p.m.	Route March – 12 miles.
3rd Day.	8.30 – 9.30 a.m.	Physical and Bayonet Training.
	9.30 – 10.30 a.m.	Company Drill.
	10.30 – 12. 0 noon.	Sections in use of own weapons.
	12. 0 – 12.30 p.m.	Gas Drill.
4th Day.	do.	do.
5th Day.	8.30 – 12.30 p.m.	Platoon in the attack; ending with Ceremonial.
6th Day.	8.30 – 12.30 p.m.	Company in the Attack; ending with Ceremonial.

Organised Games every afternoon 2.0 – 4.30 p.m.
Lectures, 6.0 – 6.30 p.m. by Platoon Commanders.
Signallers continue training and carrying out practice
of Forward Intercommunication on 5th Day.

****

THIRD WEEK.

1st Day.	8.30 – 9.30 a.m.		Physical and Bayonet Training.
	9.30 – 12.30 p.m.		Battalion Drill.
2nd Day.	8.30 – 2. 0 p.m.		Route March – 16 miles.
			Musketry.
			Tactical Exercise.
3rd Day.	8.30 – 9.30 a.m.		Physical and Bayonet Training.
	9.30 & 12. 0 a.m.		Musketry
			Tactical Exercise.
4th Day.	8.30 – 9.30 a.m.		Physical and Bayonet Training.
	9.30 – 12.30 p.m.		Outpost Scheme.
5th Day.	8.30 – 9.30 a.m.		Physical and Bayonet Training.
	9.30 – 10. 0 a.m.		Musketry.
	10. 0 – 12. 0 noon.		Battalion Drill.
	10. 0 – 12.30 p.m.		Gas Drill.
6th Day.	8.30 – 12.30 p.m.		Route March – 12 miles.

****

Organised Games every afternoon 2 p.m. to 4.30 p.m.
Lectures, 6 p.m. to 6.30 p.m. by Company Commanders.

****

Major,
Commanding, 2nd Line 8th (Irish) Bn. Liverpool Regt

1st September, 1917.

SECRET.   APPENDIX VII   Copy No. 1
                            PATROL ORDERS
                     by Major F.H.Bowring, Commanding.
                            7th Battalion.
                         5-9-17

1. **INTENTION.**   Tonight at 9-30 p.m. a party will patrol the enemy
                    trenches entering Front Line at Point N.9.d.25.10.

2. **OBJECT.**   To obtain Identification.

3. **INFORMATION.** Enemy Listening Post may be encountered at N.9.d.00.25
                    if not there it will possibly be at either N.9.c.S.1 or
                    N.9.d.45.15. The road running S.E. from the point of
                    entry is almost obliterated for a distance of about 50 yds
                    The Farm on Road at N.15.b.70.65 is almost completely in
                    ruins.
                    The neighbourhood of FARMS DE DELAPORTE, ORCHARD FARM and
                    ORCHARD HOUSE have been previously raided and no
                    opposition met with.
                    The pond across N.K.L. is in good condition, has ditch
                    on south side, trees on both sides.
                    Ground in places off road, swampy, bad going.

4. **TROOPS.**   1 Officer, 15 Other Ranks.
                    1 N.C.O. and two men to keep communication and act as
                    Supporting Party.

5. **ACTION.**   At 9-30 p.m. Party will leave our front line at N.9.c.55.72
                    bear along road S.E. entering the enemy trench at
                    N.9.d.25.10. Here they will leave the party to keep
                    communication on the parapet.
                    The remainder will follow road (which at this point is
                    badly broken up, so will work on compass bearing 158)
                    as far as point N.15.b.80.75 where tramlines meet the road.
                    Continue along the tramlines for about 200 yards where
                    there are a number of trees on left of road, here they
                    will be in wait for three hours.
                    Should it be possible to obtain Identification on
                    entering the party will at once return or any other time
                    as soon as identification has been obtained.
                    The party will return by the same route as they went out.
                    The party left in the enemy parapet will consist of
                    1 N.C.O. and five men.
                    The Supporting Party of 1 N.C.O. and 2 men will remain
                    in front line ready to go to the assistance of the
                    Patrol should they meet difficulties in getting back.

6. **EQUIPMENT.**   All ranks will wear the universal tunic, puttees,
                    Box Respirators, Steel Helmets and will carry rifle,
                    bayonet, bandolier, 2 Mills No. 5 Bombs.
                    Officer will carry luminous compass, luminous watch,
                    whistle and revolver.
                    Care must be taken that men carry no Identification
                    on them.

                                                    Captain & Adjt.,
                                                        "H" Bn.

            Copies 1 & 2 171st Bde.   Copy No. 3 Right Bn.
            Copy No. 4 O.C. "A" Coy.   Copy No. 5 O.C. "B" Coy.
            Copy No. 6 O.C. "C" Coy.   Copy No. 7 File.
                                       Copy No. 8 File.

Near FLEURBAIX on night of 5/6th September, 1917, 2nd Lieut. J.A.Free M.C. was in command of a patrol which had been sent out in order to secure identification, and discovered a German working party about 70 strong in the enemy support line. He detached a party to either flank in the hopes of cutting off some of the enemy, and accompanied by one N.C.O. went forward himself to reconnoitre.

On encountering an enemy post of 10 men, he and the N.C.O. with him opened fire, inflicting several casualties, and putting some of the enemy to flight. They then retired a few yards, reloaded some and again entered the post and took two prisoners who surrendered on being threatened. 2nd Lieut. Free then withdrew his patrol without suffering any casualties. It was due to this Officer's courage and prompt action that the object of the patrol was achieved.
....

WAR DIARY
or
INTELLIGENCE SUMMARY
(Erase heading not required.)

for Oct. 1917
2/8 Liverpool Regt

Vol 9

Place	Date	Hour	Summary of Events and Information	Remarks and references to Appendices
Tents	16/10/17		Battalion Supply Officers. 10. O.R. 985	R
	17/10/17			
	18/10/17		Battalion. Export Training carried out	
	19/10/17		How How Took to look Redon on the Munches	Apl 5/4
			Here the Motor transport from took north to Pron Area (Racecourse Camp)	
Pron Routes	23/10/17		Battalion moves from Area by Rail to Halalsy Area Entrd at Pron Area 50% of the 38% and proceed on to advanced Area due for XIV Corps. Re inforcement Camp. Battalion then takes L 33% to proceed onto line	Apl 2/R CC 36 R
Halalsy Area (Advanced)	26/10/17		Remainder of Batt'n proceed to Houston Camp. Shongie - R Road	9 R

1:10,000 K.I. Parts of 20 S.W. 4 / 20 S.E. 3 EDITION 2.

Scale. 1:10,000.

WAR DIARY
or
INTELLIGENCE SUMMARY

(Erase heading not required.)

for Oct. 1917

Instructions regarding War Diaries and Intelligence Summaries are contained in F.S. Regs., Part II. and the Staff Manual respectively. Title Pages will be prepared in manuscript.

Place	Date	Hour	Summary of Events and Information	Remarks and references to Appendices
South Camp	24/10/17		Bns of Battalion WALES in the line for up the support of 1st 17th Batt at Eagle Trench, with Batt H.Q. at Bombed Castle Gate. (Reference Map Bombed fm.)	R Relief completed from En 3
South Bank	26/10/17	10 am	Batt. 3 attacked. Batt moved up & took over front line from 139th Bde B Coy with Rifle & D Coy Lewis gun to fall in to C Coy to Hay Bank on anything up HQ Taylor House (Bombed fm) be attached to amp. HQ to front line - return to Bath relieved by 2/5 K.L.R. (Ref 28 N.W. & 11 a S.T) Stondstone Camp.	That En 1 That En 2
Stondstone	27/10			
Hipdolote Camp	28/10/17		Move to Hadsean Camp about 10 miles nearer to the coast.	
Howien Camp	30/10/17	9 am	Bn into support in Eagle Trench.	
Eagle Trench	31/10/17	10 am	Bn up to Front Line.	

E Burrough Lieut-Colonel
COMMANDING 2nd/7th (IRISH) BN. "THE KING'S" L'POOL REGT.

2/8th Battn. King's Liverpool Regiment
WAR DIARY for November 1917.
INTELLIGENCE SUMMARY.

Army Form C. 2118.

Vol 10

Place	Date	Hour	Summary of Events and Information	Remarks and references to Appendices
Lewis Farm	1/11/17		Strength 39 Off. 820 O.R.	
	2/11/17		Relieved in Front Line and proceed to Soult Camp for rest.	
Soult Camp	3/11/17			
	4/11/17		Re-organising Battalion. Officers & men from Stonalour Camp rejoin	Appendix
	5/11/17			
	6/11/17		Move to Zouafques.	
Zouafques	7/11/17 to 30/11/17		Training	
			8/11/17 Officers & O.R. rejoined from Reinforcement Camp.	
	30/11/17		Strength 43 Off. 792 O.R.	10

10 ✗

[signature]
Captain
COMMANDING 2nd LINE 8th OFFICERS BN. "THE KINGS" L'POOL

SECRET.
Ref.Map.HAZEBROUCK,   MOVE ORDER No. 21.   Copy. No. ....
  Sheet 5A.   by Lieut.-Col. O.H. North, D.S.O.
1/100,000.   Commdg. 2/8th (Irish) Bn. K.L.R.   18.10.17.

APPENDIX I

1. 2/8th (Irish) Bn. K.L.R. will move from FONTES to COIN PERDU on Oct. 19th 1917.

2. Battalion will parade ready to move at 8.30 a.m. as under -

    "A" Coy. on road from Billets, head of Coy. to rest on FONTES - AIRE Road.
    "B" Coy. in front of billets.
    "C" Coy. on road from billets, head of Coy. to rest on FONTES - AIRE Road.
    "D" Coy. in rear of "C" Coy.

3. A distance of 100 yds will be maintained between each Company and Battalion Transport.

4. Circular Memorandum No. 11 "March Discipline" and amendment with reference to smoking will be strictly adhered to.

5. A billeting party of for area to be occupied on Oct. 20th consisting of 1 N.C.O. per Coy. under Lieut. E.J. Woodcock will parade at Bn. H.Q. at 7.30 a.m. sharp.
   N.C.Os. must be in possession of slip with strength of Company for billeting purposes shown thereon.
   48 hours rations will be taken.

6. Personnel of Bn. H.Q. will be attached to "B" Coy. while on march.

7. Officers' valises etc. will be at Q.M. Stores by 7.30 a.m.

8. Billets will be left clean.
   Latrines must be filled in before leaving.

9. Medical Equipment will be ready for removal by 7.30 a.m. prompt.

10. O.C. 2/2nd Wessex Field Amb. will arrange to collect cases requiring evacuating from M.O. between 7 and 7.30 a.m.

11. A Loading Party of 1 N.C.O. and 20 men of "D" Coy. will report to Q.M. at 7.45 a.m.

                                  Capt. and Adjutant,
                                 2/8th (Irish) Bn. K.L.R.

Copy. No.			
1 - C.O.		7.	M.O.
2	O.C. "A" Coy.	8	Signalling Offr.
3	"B"	9	Q.M.
4	"C"	10	War Diary.
5	"D"	11	"
6	T.O.	12	File.

SECRET.   APPENDIX I   COPY NO. 12

ADDENDA TO MOVE ORDER NO. 21
DATED 18.10.1917.

1. **DRESS.**

   Haversack on back, groundsheet under haversack, water bottle on side.
   Steel helmet with cover.

2. **MEN'S VALISES.**

   Men's valises will be stacked by companies outside Q.M.Stores by 8-25 8.25 a.m.
   Os.C.Coys. will each detail 3 men as loaders (to travel with valises) these men to report to Sergeant Fenner at Battalion Headquarters 8 a.m.

3. **BILLETS.**

   All straw on floors of billets will be swept into one pile and left in a corner of the billet.

   Captain & Adjutant,

2nd Line 8th (Izzd) ... R.

```
COPY NO. 1  C.O.
         2  O.C. "A" Coy.
         3       "B"
         4       "C"
         5       "D"
         6  T.O.
         7  M.O.
         8  Signalling Officer.
         9  Q.M.
        10  War Diary.
        11   "    "
        12  File.
```

SECRET.   MOVE ORDER NO.23   Copy No.........
Sheet 28 N.W.   by Lt-Col. C.H.North, D.S.O., Cmdg.,
Ed.6a.1/20000.   2/8th (Irish) Bn. K.L. Regt.   23.10.1917.

1. The 2/8th (Irish) Bn. K.L.R. will move from PROVEN Area to MALAKOFF Area (SOULT Camp B.23.a.1.1.) tomorrow, October 24th.
2. The Battalion (less Transport) will parade ready to move 11-45 am. and proceed by march route to PROVEN STATION where the Battn. will entrain, detraining at X ELVERDINGHE.
3. The Transport will proceed to new area under orders of Brigade Transport Officer as per table issued to Transport Officer.
4. Dress. - Full marching order, blankets carried on valise under supporting straps. Covers will be worn on steel helmets.
5. Lewis Guns will be taken on train.
6. Bicycles will go by road with Transport. O.C.Signals will see men detailed to wheel the cycles are provided with necessary rations.
7. Stretcher Bearers will parade at 11 am. outside M.O's tent and proceed under orders of Medical Officer.
8. Route to PROVEN will be via CROSS ROADS on the WATOU ROAD, 850 yards South of Brigade Headquarters.
9. 100 yards distance will be maintained between Coys. on march to PROVEN STATION, 200 yards between Coys. on arrival at new area.
10. Officers' valises will be stacked at Q.M. Stores by 8 am.
11. Cookers, Medical Equipment, will be ready for removal at 9.30 am.
12. 2 Cooks per Coy. will accompany Cookers.
13. Haversack rations will be issued for midday meal.
14. Lines will be left clean and be ready for inspection 11 a.m.

ROUTINE FOR WEDNESDAY.
        Reveille 6 a.m.   Sick Parade 8 a.m.

                        (Sgd) J.H.BRADLEY, Captain & Adjt.,
                          2/8th (Irish) Bn. K.L.R.

            COPY NO. 1 C.O.
                     2. O.C. "A" Coy.
                     3.   "B"
                     4.   "C"
                     5.   "D"
                     6 O.C.Signals.
                     7 M.O.
                     8 T.O.
                     9 Q.M.
                    10 L.G.O.
                    11 2nd in Cd.
                    12 War Diary.
                    13   "   "
                    14 File.

SECRET.   APPENDIX III   COPY NO. 9

MOVE ORDER NO. 24
by Lt.-Col. O.H.North, D.S.O. Cmdg.,
2/8th (Irish) Bn. King's L'pool Regt.   25.10.17.

The 170th Infantry Brigade is now holding the line which runs roughly from REQUETTE FARM - GRAVEL FARM - BROEMBEER REVER. V.7.b.60.45.
There are 3 Battalions is the Line and one Battalion in Support:-

RIGHT SECTION.
    2/5th L.N.L.   Battn.HQ.   FERDAN HOUSE
                                        V.19.a.75.60.

CENTRAL SECTION.
    2/4th L.N.L.R.   "   "   LOUIS FARM.
                                        U.24.c.50.95.

LEFT SECTION.
    4/5th L.N.L.R.   "   "   OLGA HOUSES.
                                        U.18.b.55.15.

SUPPORT BATTN.
    2/5 th K.O.R.L.   "   "   DOUBLE COTTS
                                        U.23.d.30.20.

1. Today, Oct. 25th, the 2/8th K.L.R. less Officers and men detailed to stay at Transport will move into EAGLE TRENCH in U.23.b. & d.

2. The Battn. will parade ready to move 3.15 pm. and will proceed by road running North-East past Camp, thence by duckboard track which commences some 200 yards up the road to Canal at BARD CAUSEWAY B.18.d.9.3. where R.E.Stores will be drawn, across the canal, then to EAGLE TRENCH by Track "B".

3. DRESS. Full marching order, waterbottles filled, box respirators at alert position, rations.

4. Battn. will move at 200 yards interval between coys. West of Canal, 100 yards between half-platoons East of Canal.

5. Bn. Hdqrs. will be established at DOUBLE COTTS U.23.d.30.20.

6. Lines will be left clean.

7. Runners for Hdqrs and Coy. Signallers will report to their respective Os.C. by 3 p.m.

                                              Captain & Adjt.,
                                      2/8th (Irish) Bn. K.L.R.

COPY NO. 1 C.O.
        2 O.C. "A" Coy.
        3   "   "B"
        4   "C"
        5   "D"
        6 O.C. Signals.
        7 War Diary.
        8   "   "
        9 File.

SECRET.   Copy No........

              2/8th Bn. K.L.R. ORDER   Appendix 1.
                   for Move to
                    ZOUAFQUES.   5.11.17.

1. The Battalion, less transport will parade ready to move 10.50 a.m. entraining at ELVERDINGHE 12 noon.
   Transport will move in accordance with table issued to Transport Officer.

2. One cook per Company will be detailed to accompany Cookers.

3. Lines will be left clean.

4. One N.C.O. per Company will accompany lorry and parade by O.C.S. 9.45 a.m. reporting to Lieut. E.J. Woodcock.

5. An interval of 100 yards will be maintained between Coys.

                                        (Sgd) J.H. BRADLEY, Captain & Adjt.,
                                               2/8th (Irish) Bn. K. L. R.

                COPY NO. 1 C.O.
                        2 2nd in Cd.
                        3 O.C. "A" Coy.
                        4   "B"
                        5   "C"
                        6   "D"
                        7 O.C. Signals.
                        8 M.O.
                        9 Spare.
                      10 War Diary.
                      11   "   "
                      12 File.

SECRET. 　　　　　　　　　　　　　　　　　　　　　　　　　　Copy No..........

Map Ref: 　　　　　　2nd Line 8th (Irish) Bn. 　　　　Appendix 1.
Sheet 5a. 　　　　　King's Liverpool Regiment. 　　　　5.11.17
HAZEBROUCK. 　　　　　MOVE - WARNING ORDER.

1. 2/8th (Irish) Bn. K.L.R. will move to ZOUAFQUES tomorrow, November 6th.

2. Train arrangements and portion of Transport necessary to move by road will be notified later.

3. Dress. Full marching order - blankets to be carried by men.

4. Officers' kits, Mess Boxes, Orderly Room Stores, Medical Officer's equipment, and Camp Kettles necessary to provide meals in case Cookers do not arrive along with Battalion and Breakfast ration will be stacked on side of road by C.C.S. by 9.30 a.m.

5. Loading Party of 1 N.C.O. and 3 men per Coy. will report to Lieut. E.J. Woodcock at C.C.S. 9.45 a.m.

6. Meals:- Breakfast 6.30 a.m., Dinner 10.15 a.m. Tea Ration to be carried by men.

7. Sick Parade 8.30 a.m.

8. Bicycles will accompany Battalion on Train.

　　　　　　　　　　　　　　　　　　　　　　J. Bradley
　　　　　　　　　　　　　　　　　　　　　Captain & Adjt.,
　　　　　　　　　　　　　　　　　　　2/8th (Irish) Bn. K.L.R.

```
COPY NO. 1  C.O.
         2  2nd in Cd.
         3  O.C. "A" Coy.
         4       "B"
         5       "C"
         6       "D"
         7  M.O.
         8  O.C. Signals.
         9  T.O.
        10  Q.M.
        11  Spare.
        12  War Diary.
        13    "    "
        14  File.
```

Headquarters,
    57th Division.
        .....

        Herewith War Diary of this Unit for
the month of December, 1917.

                    J H Bowring
                            Major,
            Cmdg., 2/8th (Irish) Bn. K. L. R.

31.12.1917.

WAR DIARY
or
INTELLIGENCE SUMMARY.
(Erase heading not required.)

2/5 Liverpool R

Place	Date	Hour	Summary of Events and Information	Remarks and references to Appendices
Busseboom	1/2/17		Strent R. offr 23 O.R. other Ranks 492.	
	5/2/17		Had Qrs. Bugeons to Paddington Camp. Coys One to Paddington Camp.	
Shover	9/2/17		Shover area to Busseboom Camp. Cam. Cuban Camp.	
			Coy Swam at Cuban Camp to Right Sector of Brigade Front	
Busseboom	20/2/17		Relieved 2/4 K.L.R. in right sub-sector of Hulluch Wed Sector	
Line	24/2/17		At 4.30 A.M. enemy exploded front line between No.1 Crater near shaft	
			14 a.1 & the land through WITIRENE CRASSIER Y.1.a.24½. A 5.10 A.M. a barrage	
			of rifle & enemy shells on line No. 1 + 2 craters which he succeeded in	
			occupying. 2/5 Lee B.C. Bn. Passes 7 3 O.R. being captured	
			missing. At 8.15 P.M. D. Coy. of same under Capt. G.H. Sutherland	
			counter attacked enemy on Line captured but failed to close out	
			the enemy. 2/5 L.H. Johnson 2 O.R. Rifles kld. killed	
	25/2/17		12 O.R. wounded & Capt. Mrs. Bucknall rounds 2 O.R. and O.R. Heap, Berry	
	26/2/17		R & D Coys relieved by 2 Coys 2/ 95 R.S.L.T.	
	27/2/17		Bath relieved by 1/95 South Lancs & proceeds to Brunswick Camp	

Army Form C. 2118.

WAR DIARY
or
INTELLIGENCE SUMMARY.
(Erase heading not required.)

Instructions regarding War Diaries and Intelligence Summaries are contained in F. S. Regs., Part II. and the Staff Manual respectively. Title pages will be prepared in manuscript.

Place	Date	Hour	Summary of Events and Information	Remarks and references to Appendices
Brouay	1/24/17		Left Crossroad Camp for Camp du Sterr Vlees	Ref Appx
Camp du Sterr Vlees	30/9/17		Gave orders Battle at Therouanne for one night	Appendixed
Therouanne	31/9/17		Gave into De Seule	5a / VD OM/2
	3/7/40		Batt. Strength O. 26 O.R. 574	

J.A. Armstrong
Major,
Cmdg., 2/8th (Irish) Bn. K. L. R.

Headquarters,
    57th Division.

    I beg to forward herewith War Diary for
month of January 1918.

                                Lieut.-Colonel,
            Commdg. 8th (Irish) Bn. K. L. R.

1.2.18.

2/8th (Irish) Batt.
King's Liverpool Regiment

Army Form C. 2118.

WAR DIARY
INTELLIGENCE SUMMARY

(Erase heading not required.)

Instructions regarding War Diaries and Intelligence Summaries are contained in F. S. Regs., Part II. and the Staff Manual respectively. Title pages will be prepared in manuscript.

Place	Date	Hour	Summary of Events and Information	Remarks and references to Appendices
Re Seule Camp	1/1/18		Battn Strength 38 Officers and 693 Other Ranks. Total Strength 40 O. 879 O.R.	
	2/1/18		Moved to Billet in Laundry at Erquinghem — Ref Sht 36 NW. H.5.a.50.70	
Erquinghem	3/1/18		Moved to Billets in Armentieres. Ref Sht 36 NW. B.30.d. central (2nd Bn Billets)	
Armentieres	4/1/18		Relieved 2/5 K.L.R. in L'Epinette Sector.	
L'Epinette	5			
	6			
	7			
	8			
	9		Enemy quiet during tour. Slight increase in Artillery Activity + also T.M. during last tour. Quiet in Sector, nothing in particular	
	10.1.18		to report. Enemy fired about 20 Trench mortar shots	
	11		into our line. Leeds morning strafe seen.	
	12		Casualties O.R. 1 K. 3 W.	
	13/1/18		Relieved by 2/9 K.L.R. Moved to Pont Herache Camp. Bn a - 1 1. Sht 36 NW.	
	14			
	15			
	16		Training + Working parties	
	17			
	18			
	19			
	20			

Army Form C. 2118.

WAR DIARY
or
INTELLIGENCE SUMMARY.
(Erase heading not required.)

Instructions regarding War Diaries and Intelligence Summaries are contained in F. S. Regs., Part II. and the Staff Manual respectively. Title pages will be prepared in manuscript.

Place	Date	Hour	Summary of Events and Information	Remarks and references to Appendices
Étaples	21		Relieved 1/9 K.L.R. in subsidiary line. C.&D. Coys. in front line	
	22		1/6 K.L.R. trenches relieved C. & D. Coys under command 1/5 K.L.R.	
	23		L'épinette sub-sector	
	24		Relieved 1/5 K.L.R. in L'épinette sub-sector	
Armentières	25		K.E. Very active at night	
Louvrette	26		Shell shelling K.E. very active at night	
	27		Relieved 1/ Welsh -1/4 Bn in Louvrette sub sector. Enemy aeroplane working from St Cyprien to Louvrette. Ex-otherwise quiet during the Month	
	28		Relieved by 1/4 R.W.Fus. Bn. Rev'd Loos Left	
Noeux Camp	28		Marching forward by Batt. in Byr's bivouac Tent	
	29		Resting South of Mont St. Eloi	
	30		Battalion Baths 1st & 2nd Coys Remounts drawing clothing, Linen, gas Yeor. O. Ro'd King	
	31		Reconstruction of Coys, 1st 2nd Lines. Fur O Ro'd Col R.E. Heath falling in and re-mounted 2nd line Comm: emerald of 2W: Bath. over to Col D.W. Mack, D.S.O. of 3rd Bn Kings D.S.O. the Bath, well in return to Comd 2nd Bn & R.W. Fus., D.K.L.R. Batt. Strength 52 offrs ~ 927 O.R.	

J A Beard LIEUT-COLONEL
COMMANDING 2nd LINE 816 (IRISH) BN. THE KING'S L'POOL REGT.

Headquarters,
    57th Division.

    Herewith original War Diary for this Battalion for the month of February 1918.

                                         Major,
            Commdg. 8th (Irish) Bn. K. L. R.

9. 3. 18.

www.ingramcontent.com/pod-product-compliance
Lightning Source LLC
Chambersburg PA
CBHW081438160426
43193CB00013B/2322